My Story,
Sepsis Raw and Real

Marguerite Henderson

Mikamme Books

Published in 2020 by Mikamme Books

Copyright © Marguerite Henderson 2020

Marguerite Henderson has asserted her right to be identified as the author
of this Work in accordance with the Copyright, Designs
and Patents Act 1988

ISBN Paperback: 978-1-8381423-0-8
Ebook: 978-1-8381423-1-5

A CIP catalogue copy of this book can be found in the British Library.

Published with the help of Indie Authors World
www.indieauthorsworld.com

IndieAuthors
World

ACKNOWLEDGEMENTS

I would like to take this opportunity to thank all my family and friends who encouraged me to write my story. To Florence my friend for reading my book once completed, and encouraging me to get it published, as I hadn't been sure it was worthy of reading.

I would also like to thank my sister Dianne and my brother in law Trevor for proof reading my book and Alexander Henderson (Photographer) for taking the photo on the back cover.

Lastly, I would like to thank Kim and Sinclair of Indie Authors World Publishers, for helping me through the process of publishing my story and making seeing my book in print a reality.

DEDICATION

This book is dedicated to my amazing physiotherapist, Kerry Murphy, who was by my side throughout my journey. She has no idea of how her support helped me cope and remain strong, when many a time, I felt like giving up. She believed in me from the word go and I learned very quickly, that I could trust her implicitly. She was always honest and frank and told me exactly how it was, even though it was hard for me to hear at times. She also gave me hope and the ability to recognise what I was capable of, and helped me achieve success after success.

Kerry, I know your commitment to me and the support you gave my family, went well beyond what your role as my physio required. Your determination to keep working with me after I was discharged from hospital was so appreciated, as I know it was not normal NHS procedure. But you knew I needed to continue my physio sessions to be able to build on my mobility and be all that I could be, and I am so appreciative of you for going the extra mile to help make that happen.

Thank you, Kerry, for being my friend, the person I could confide in and be honest with, when I needed it most. The person that made me laugh and see the funny side of the situation I found myself in, recognising the need for humour to keep me strong, when it could have been so easy for me to focus on feeling sorry for myself.

I feel you know me better than I know myself and I know the relationship I have with you is one that no one could replace. I will be eternally grateful for all you've done for me, in so many ways, but mostly for helping me achieve being able to walk again. I never thought, when I had my limbs removed, that that would be possible and I know to begin with, you didn't either. But you quickly recognised there was hope and you made it your goal to make it happen. You made me see that too, and together we made it a reality.

Contracting sepsis was a horrific experience and changed my life forever, but it led to me meeting you. You will always have a special place in my heart and the memories I have of our time together, will remain with me forever.

PROLOGUE - INTRODUCTION

At the beginning of 2018, I was working full time in a job I loved, as a Family Support Worker with the Education Department of my local council. I also did relief work at a couple of Residential Children's Homes near to where I live and enjoyed working in them, as it was so different from my role as a Family Support Worker, but just as rewarding. Doing relief work also meant I was comfortable financially. As a single parent, I had struggled financially, bringing up two daughters on my own, so life had been hard at times.

Kim, my eldest daughter who was aged 26, had married in 2016 and she and Sean, her husband, had two daughters, Erin, aged 6 and Gracie aged 1. Kim and Sean had bought our family home in December 2015, the bungalow my ex-husband and I had built in 1990. I had become fed up with spending my free time doing house work in a house that was now too big for my needs. The garden was large and needed weekly maintenance, a chore I had once enjoyed, but recently found tiresome and constricting, as it meant I had little relaxation time, which I had begun to crave.

I had moved around the corner to a smaller bungalow, with my younger daughter Emma, aged 18, and had spent the last two years renovating it inside and out. A new kitchen had just been installed, the last job to be done, with me planning then to relax more and have some free time to enjoy life.

I was an independent, hands on person, who liked interior design challenges, so had enjoyed putting my stamp on my new home, even down to painting canvases for my living room wall, as I couldn't find pictures that went well with my decor. I enjoyed creative activities. One of my hobbies was sewing and I always had sewing jobs on the go, whether it was alterations or making curtains and Roman Blinds for family, friends or myself. I would also make fascinators or corsages when required.

I am the youngest of five children, even though it was by only twenty minutes, as I have a twin brother. I also have two older sisters and an older brother. My parents are no longer living, but they had installed in us all the importance of family, so I had a close relationship with all my siblings and their families. I also had close relationships with my aunties, uncles and cousins and would meet up with them at family events. I felt privileged to be surrounded by a large family, with me having so many

Figure 1; Me, Christmas 2017

memories of happy times.

I had a great circle of friends and enjoyed socialising with them, usually at my house on Friday nights - WINE NIGHT. I also enjoyed weekend breaks and went away with friends at the beginning of December every year to enjoy spending time together before the onset of Christmas.

I enjoyed holidays in the sun and planned to go away to somewhere exotic that summer, to relax by the pool and soak up the atmosphere in the evenings.

I was in a fairly new relationship, which was going well, and life was good. The holiday planned for that summer was to be our first holiday together.

My life as it was, was about to change. I was about to begin a journey that was at times unbearable to cope with and that would have drastic effects which would massively change me forever. It would also affect my immediate family, who would experience trauma beyond belief, with their lives also changing unimaginably. I'm so enormously proud of them for how they have coped. They have shown immense strength and resilience and have been by my side every step of the way, focussing on caring for me and making my life as best as it could be. We'd always had a close bond, with there being only the three of us for so long as I had separated from their father in 2005. Incredibly, that bond is now even stronger and I love them so much.

Figure 2; October 2017, Emma's 18th Birthday

CHAPTER 1

How My Story Begins

On Sunday the 25th February I was doing relief work at a local Residential Home when I discovered a small 1-centimetre long paper cut on my right index finger. I had no idea how I had acquired it. The next morning, I noticed that a small, blue, bruised blister had appeared in the middle of the cut, approximately 1/2 centimetre in circumference, which I thought looked a bit odd. However, the cut was not giving me any pain or discomfort and I went off to work as normal, deciding that I would go to the pharmacy during my lunch break to inquire if I could get cream to treat it.

I spoke to the pharmacist in the chemist near the school I had been working in that morning and was advised to make an appointment with my GP, which I did from the pharmacy car park. I got an appointment for around 4pm on Tuesday, the next day. I then went back to work for the afternoon and then picked up Emma, my youngest daughter, from college, as I always did on a Monday, before heading home.

On arriving home, I made dinner and after we'd eaten, I spent the evening painting the woodwork in my newly installed kitchen, which was near completion. I was so excited about seeing it finished. I stopped painting around 10:30pm and headed to bed, feeling tired, but contented. Little did I know that I'd never be able to use my new kitchen as I'd hoped to, because of what happened next.

*

The next morning, Tuesday the 27th February, I woke up feeling lousy, aching all over and no way well enough to go to work. I phoned the office to inform them I was unwell and would not be in that day. I then phoned the doctors' surgery to cancel the appointment I had made the day before and rearranged it for around 4pm on Wednesday, the next day. Whilst speaking to the receptionist about how unwell I was feeling, she informed me there was a virus going around and maybe that was what was wrong with me. I then spent the day in bed, hoping to feel better the following day. Emma came into my room that evening and asked if she could light a perfumed candle for me, as there was a horrible smell. I remember saying, "Thanks Emma!" for showing me so little sympathy when I was feeling so lousy. A few weeks later when talking to Emma, she told me that the smell in the room that night was the same one she had smelled when her gran was dying four years earlier, but she hadn't recognised that until after I had arrived in ICU. (Intensive Care Unit). I often think, how must she have felt when she realised what the smell was? She must have been so scared with that knowledge, frightened that that was my destiny.

*

The next day, Wednesday the 28th February, I woke up feeling even more unwell, with pain in my right arm and under my armpit. I couldn't understand how I'd hurt them, not having been out of bed since the Monday evening. Sometime during that morning, the doctors' surgery called me to ask if I still needed my appointment for later that day, as they were cancelling or rescheduling all appointments, due to the severe snowy weather. As I had been in bed since the Monday, I had no idea it had been snowing, or how severe the snow was.

Anyway, I said that I still needed an appointment, as I still needed the doctor to look at my cut finger. I explained that I was feeling even more unwell than I had been the day before and made them aware that I now had a sore arm and under arm and that I couldn't account for. After the phone called ended, I remained in bed dozing in and out of sleep.

At one point, I remember my boyfriend phoning me to ask how I was and telling him how unwell I was feeling. I found out later, that he had called Emma after talking to me, to let her know that something was far wrong with me, as I had been slurring my words during our phone conversation.

By late afternoon, I felt so unwell that I contacted the doctors' surgery to make them aware of how unwell I was feeling and to inform them that I wouldn't be able to make my appointment at 4pm. I was informed that there were no doctors in attendance, as they had all gone home, due to the severe weather. THE BEAST FROM THE EAST had arrived in Scotland. I remember just ending the call and then thinking, "What will I do now?" A short time later my phone rang and it was a doctor from the surgery, stating she was calling from her home. She told me that if I had called earlier, she would have made a house call to me on her way home. I explained to her how unwell I was feeling and that my arm and under arm were sore, which I could not explain. She then advised me, that if I still felt unwell at 6pm, to contact NHS 24 for assistance.

After ending the call, I remember feeling fear and panic, recognising that how ill I was feeling wasn't normal. I knew that I urgently needed help.

I called Kim, my eldest daughter, explaining how unwell I felt and how the doctor had advised me to contact NHS 24, asking her if she had the contact details. It was then that Sean, my son-in-law, told Kim to tell me that he was coming to take me to A & E (Accident & Emergency). He stated that due to the severe weather, waiting until 6pm to phone NHS 24, would probably mean I would have a long time to wait for help and he recognised I needed to get to hospital as soon as possible. I remember I found getting out of bed difficult, as I felt so weak and disorientated. I tried to put clothes on, but was too weak to achieve this. Kim arrived a short time later and advised me to stay in my pyjamas and helped me put my coat and boots on. Sean arrived after dropping off my granddaughters at his parents' house, so that they would be looked after while we went to the hospital. I remember him coming into my room and saying, "Oh my god!" He later informed me that on arriving to take me to hospital, my face had been grey and my lips had been blue. I needed support to walk and remember the snow falling heavily as I walked unsteadily to the car, unaware that it would be the last time I'd ever walk on my own feet. Emma was at her friend's house, so we picked her up en route and she accompanied us to the hospital too.

*

The weather was horrendous on the way to the Victoria Hospital in Kirkcaldy, with heavy snow falling throughout the journey. There was very little traffic on the road and I felt really drowsy. Sean kept telling me to keep my eyes open and not to fall asleep. I remember thinking, "Why is he saying that?" and now I realise that it was because I looked so ill that he was frightened of me falling asleep, in case I didn't wake up again. As we reached Kirkcaldy, I asked Sean to stop the car and I leaned out of the door and was violently sick. I hadn't been sick before this and recognised that this was an indication that my health was deteriorating.

On arriving at the hospital, Sean ran to get me a wheelchair, because I was too weak to walk. As he wheeled me into A & E, I remember saying to him that I couldn't cope if I had to wait to be seen, as I felt so awful. He replied that I wasn't to worry, as 'I wouldn't be waiting in the waiting room'. I had no idea at the time that Sean was saying this because of how seriously ill he thought I was. I remember Sean, Kim and I arriving at the A & E Reception window and speaking to the receptionist, but I don't remember going through the door into the Casualty department, or of what happened next.

CHAPTER 2

Casualty

I've been told that on arrival in A & E, I was examined and blood tests were done. My blood pressure was low, so I was given an intravenous drip to provide me with fluids. I had pain in the right side of my neck and the doctors were concerned that the infection in my finger had spread up my arm, so I had a CT Scan of my neck, to look for signs of spreading infection. The doctors remained concerned, as even after being given fluids intravenously, my blood pressure remained low, so I was started on strong antibiotics intravenously.

Whilst in A & E, other members of the family were contacted. Sean went to collect my eldest brother and my auntie and uncle, with my twin brother and nephew arriving also. I've been told, their journeys to and from the hospital that night had been very dangerous and difficult, due to the snow conditions, but recognising how ill I was, they wanted to be with me and to support my own little family. A visitor's room was allocated to them as there were too many people to all be with me at the same time.

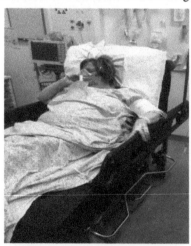

Figure 3; Me in Casualty. Although I can't remember being there, my daughters have informed me, that I was lucid and conscious at this stage.

I was taken to HDU (High Dependency Unit), so that I could be given medication for my low blood pressure. Once I was settled, my family left to go home. It was now the early hours of Thursday morning, the 1st of March.

However, my condition continued to deteriorate and the ICU doctors were brought in. A Central Line (a large drip) was inserted into the vein in my neck, enabling me to be given stronger medication, as my blood pressure remained dangerously low. But it continued to remain low and due to the blood supply to my organs being poor, I'd began to accumulate toxins in my blood. Normally my liver and kidneys would have removed any toxins.

It was then that the decision was made to move me to ICU (Intensive Care Unit).

CHAPTER 3

ICU

Kim contacted HDU on the Thursday morning to inquire how I was and was informed that I hadn't had a good night. She presumed this meant I hadn't slept well. Kim, Sean and Emma had set off to drive to the hospital, having to divert from their normal route, due to road blocks caused by the severe weather conditions. At one point, they got stuck in a snow drift and had to be pulled out by a 4 x 4 vehicle. Kim received a call from my older brother, just as they arrived in the hospital car park, telling her that I was being transferred to ICU because my health was deteriorating.

Over the next few hours my condition rapidly deteriorated, despite increased levels of organ support, and the decision was made to put me into an induced coma to help let my body rest.

Even though I have no recollection of my time in ICU, I do remember being told I was being put into a coma and telling Kim and Emma, not to worry, as I was going to wake up. And I did. I thought I was dreaming and it wasn't until I was fully awake that I became aware that it wasn't a dream, but reality.

Before I was put into an induced coma, Kim had telephoned my auntie and uncle (my mum's youngest brother and sister) who had visited me the night before, so that I could speak to them. The snow conditions had prevented them from making their way to the hospital. I don't remember speaking to them, or seeing any family members who had managed to get through the snow to be with me.

A breathing tube was placed in my windpipe and I was connected to a ventilator. A line was placed in the pulse of my wrist to accurately measure my blood pressure and to allow blood samples to be taken. A tube was inserted through my nose and into my stomach, so that I could receive nutrients whilst I was sleeping and a catheter was inserted into my bladder. Another central line was inserted into the vein at the top of my leg. That allowed me to be connected to the kidney dialysis machine, to clear the toxins from my blood. Kim has spoken about her distress at being with me when the doctors had previously tried to insert this line, prior to me being in the coma. She had been really upset at seeing me in agony as the doctors tried their best to insert a line. In the end, it was inserted once I was sedated.

I was also given continuous drips of sedatives and pain killers to keep me comfortable and asleep

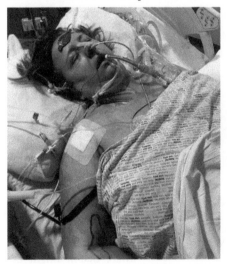

Figure 4; So many tubes to help keep me alive

Whilst in the coma, doctors performed a small operation on my arm to look for signs of spreading infection and both were clear. However, I was given a broad spectrum of antibiotics to dampen the response of infection on my immune system.

Over the next three days I was extremely ill and required the highest level of organ support. My family was warned of the possibility that I might not survive. Kim has told me that when I was put in the coma, she had never thought that I might not wake up. She had been very upset. If she had known this, she would have phoned Erin and Gracie and let me speak to them before I was put to sleep. The thought of my girls having to go through this harrowing ordeal, without me being able to give them a cuddle and help them deal with the most difficult experience they'd ever had to deal with, is so upsetting. But I've been told they coped with maturity and a strength beyond their years and I'm so proud of them.

The high level of medication I needed to fight what was now acknowledged as sepsis, and for my problematic blood pressure, led to the circulation to my extremities being very poor. The tissue was not getting enough oxygen and it became clear that my fingers and toes had been badly damaged.

Due to the severe weather, some of my close family had difficulty travelling to the hospital and those who made it there took turns to sit with me, spending the rest of their time in the family room. I've been told that I was constantly spoken to by family and staff and even though I was so unwell and they found seeing me so ill upsetting, they would joke and laugh with each other, in the hope I could hear them. Music was also played in the hope that I would respond. My family was given a note book by ICU, so that they could write messages to me when they visited. This would make me aware of what had been happening whilst I was

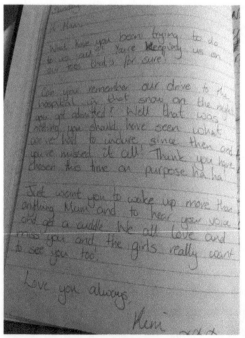

in a deep sleep. Reading it once I felt strong enough to do so was gruelling, as it made me aware of what my family had gone through.

I believe, many of my extended family and close friends visited me, aware that it might be the last time they would see me alive.

Over the next few days, the doctors managed to treat the infection effectively and as my condition improved, the support I needed from

Figure 5; Kim's message in my ICU note book

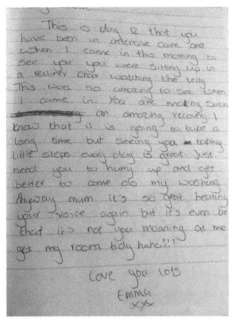

Figure 6; Emma's message in my ICUY note book

the ventilator was reduced, leading to my breathing tube being removed on the 8th of March. A few days later, my kidney dialysis was also stopped. Because I survived being so ill, when it wasn't expected that I would, my DNA has been analysed to explore if there is something present in it which gave me the ability to survive, when most people wouldn't have. Knowing this is hard for me to comprehend. To me, it highlights that it was a miracle that I survived.

My first lucid memory is when a doctor came to my bedside and spoke to me. Kim, Sean, my brother Willie and my sister-in-law, Linda, were present. It was then that he told me, that I had been the most ill person in the hospital when I was admitted and that if it wasn't for Sean, making the decision to bring me to the hospital when he did, I would have died. I'm very much aware that if I had put the phone down that day and not phoned Kim for

Figure 7; Erin's drawing in my ICU note book

19

the telephone number for NHS 24, but instead closed my eyes and gone to sleep, I would probably never have wakened up again. I would have died in my bed. That thought really scares me as it would have been Emma who found me, which is too frightening to imagine.

It's difficult for me to understand that the events of my time in ICU really happened to me. I don't remember most of it, even after I awakened from the coma. I have little recollection of being in ICU at all.

I have recently had flashbacks. I remember watching the green lights on the ceiling as I lay in a bed that felt alien. I remember dreaming that I was in a different hospital every day and feeling very scared and vulnerable, as I couldn't move or do anything for myself. I have a recollection of not being heard when I tried to speak to the nursing staff and ask for help. I now think that that was because my voice was so weak. I also have a memory of asking for my catheter bag to be removed, so that I could go to the toilet and the young nurse who was caring for me looking at me, not knowing what to do. A doctor came to explain that I needed to keep it in. Now I realise that it was practically impossible to remove it as I was attached to so many machines and there were wires everywhere, and because my legs were dying, I couldn't stand up, never mind walk on them to go to the toilet.

I remember feeling really thirsty and asking for a drink and being given sponge sticks, which were moist and were used to moisten my mouth. They didn't quench my thirst.

Another memory I have, is of my sister coming in to visit me and me telling her that I had noticed that my foot was black and asking her why this was. She never gave me an answer. Afterwards she told me that she didn't know what to say to me, so had ignored my question and changed the subject. She told me that she had been very emotional and had to stop herself from getting upset, trying not to show me that there was something wrong. She later asked a doctor how to deal with the issue of my limbs turning black should I ask her again.

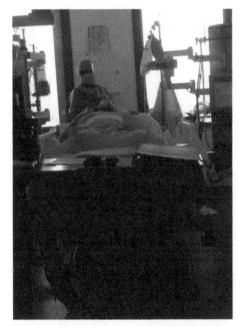

Figure 8; Me in ICU

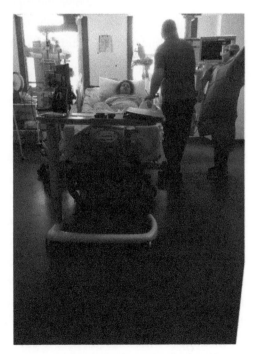

Figure 9; Feeling confused, scared and vulnerable

CHAPTER 4

HDU (The High Dependency Unit)

On the 14th of March I was moved to HDU. Even though I was more alert and lucid, I was struggling with the concept of being in hospital. I had only been a patient once before, at the age of nine, when I had had an operation to have my tonsils removed. That memory wasn't a good one and made me feel apprehensive and frightened. I was sedated with drugs and this meant I was often incoherent and not able to recognise what was reality and what were dreams from my time in ICU.

*

It was in HDU that I was informed by the doctors that I was to lose my legs and arms. They explained that due to them having to save my life through concentrating on saving my vital organs, my extremities had been damaged, and could not be saved. I was on my own when I was told this news and although my family was annoyed that they weren't there to support me, when I was told something so horrific, I think I preferred it that way. I needed to come to terms with it on my own. I needed to digest and be able to process what I'd been told, without other influences. I remember silent tears running down my face as they spoke and the doctors asking if I wanted to be left alone for a while. I nodded. They closed the curtains behind them and I sobbed. If I'm honest, I don't think it really sunk in, or that I really was able to comprehend the enormity of what I had just been told. However, I did think, they'd have been better letting me slip away whilst in a coma. Why would they think anyone living without all four limbs was justifiable? I did feel that I was living in a surreal world and was coping by just going through the motions. I do think now that my brain was helping me cope by making me react in this way, and it would continue to be like this for many weeks to come.

I was still very ill and a nurse was assigned to care for me on a one to one basis. I was attached to a lot of machines and I couldn't move my body. I had a catheter inserted, which I hated, but which I had to learn to accept, as I would have it for a few weeks to come before it would be eventually removed.

*

As my body felt like lead, the nursing staff had to move me from side to side in my bed to give me a bed bath and change my hospital gown. They also had to brush my teeth and hair. To move me up the bed, they had to use what they call a slide sheet, which was a large sheet made from red lining material. Two nurses were needed to do this task. Each nurse would stand on either side of my bed and move me back and forwards from side to side, until I was lying on top of the sheet. It would then be pulled by the two nurses, with it sliding me back up the bed. An Argentinian nurse looked after me whilst in HDU and she made me laugh. Every time she used the slide sheet under me she got an electric shock, leading to her doing a dance around my bed. There was also a really caring Nursing Assistant and as I could not sit up, being so weak and unable to use my hands, she fed me my breakfast. She would break up a piece of toast into small pieces, enabling me to eat it. She also gave me drinks from a beaker. I always felt thirsty, but could only drink small amounts at a time. She was so patient with me. I remember that there was chilled water in HDU and it was so thirst quenching.

I had no appetite and my family and friends would bring me in fruits, such as mango and pineapple, to encourage me to eat, as my taste for food was poor. Food which was juicy and flavoursome was the only thing that would tempt me to eat. My big sister Dianne seemed to me, even then, to be on a mission to encourage me to be pro-active and fight my illness, even when I didn't want to. She would try and get me to eat anything she had brought in, even if it was only a few mouthfuls. Fluids also felt tasteless. Many types of juices were brought in, in an attempt to get me to drink more. It was weird, as my taste buds must have continually changed. One juice would feel flavoursome for a time and then I'd no longer enjoy it. I remember one day my friend's daughter came to visit me and brought me, Ribena. I really enjoyed its strong flavour and she left me two bottles. It led to me getting an influx of Ribena, as my visitors were all keen to see me drinking more. However, my liking of it didn't last long and I was then back to trying to find a drink I liked again. My drinking issue continued for a few weeks to come. I could not drink fizzy juice, as I found it frothy in my mouth. It would be weeks before I was able to drink it without feeling nauseous.

I remember my friends visiting me while in HDU. They had visited me in ICU, but I didn't remember that. I remember thinking when they visited that they looked sad, and I recognised by how they acted, that I was still very ill and that they were trying hard to be brave and act normally. They have told me since my recovery, that visiting me was very hard and emotional for them, as it was so difficult seeing me so ill and knowing I was going to lose my limbs. They didn't want me to pick up on how they were feeling and scare me, recognising how hard the journey in front of me was going to be. They would help me have a drink to quench my thirst and they too, would bring me food and encourage me to eat. I remember on one occasion, my friend Florence bringing me in a roll filled with cooked ham. She'd cut it in two and helped me eat one half of it. Although I couldn't eat more than the one half, I remember it being really tasty. Having enjoyed it so much when my appetite was poor, was a positive.

My friends would also update me on what was happening in the outside world, talking about everyday things that were not related to the present situation I found myself in. I would try hard to stay awake when I had visitors, but sometimes I was too tired to keep my eyes open.

During my time in High Dependency, I constantly felt weak and lethargic and I just lay in the bed. Even talking was too much effort most of the time. I felt unable to concentrate for any length of time, not even to watch some television. Mind you, Day Time television isn't something I usually watched, so it didn't entice me.

*

Not long after I arrived in HDU, I met two people, who at that time, I didn't realise would be with me every day during my stay in hospital, listening to my needs and helping me every step of the way on my long road to recovery. When I first met them, I was just going through the motions and just accepting everything that happened around me. I didn't really understand why they were talking to me, as I didn't really understand what had happened to me, or what lay ahead. I didn't take on board what their roles were going to be in supporting me. Looking back now, I see them both as my saviours and I owe them so much. They helped bring me back to life in so many ways, much more than their jobs required. They helped me find ME again. But that would be a long way along my journey of recovery.

*

KERRY would by my physiotherapist, who I'd learn to trust explicitly and who would be my rock and shoulder to cry on. She would be the person who would motivate me and give me hope. She would have faith in my ability to have the strength and determination not to give up, and inspire me to believe in myself and remain positive. She enabled me to strive to achieve my goal to walk again, and I did. I believe that the bond I developed with Kerry at quite an early stage in my journey to recovery, was a bond made of trust. I would not be walking today without her support. She is the most amazing physiotherapist, who achieves miracles. She gave me back my life and made it worth living, and for that I am eternally grateful. Yes, the long road to achieve this would not be easy, but she had faith in me and helped me have faith in myself.

*

TRACEY was to be my OT (Occupational Therapist), who would problem-solve to help me achieve goals regarding everyday tasks. She would listen to my needs and then make it her goal to help me achieve them. Mind you, Tracey seemed to always come to see me when I was in the shower or toilet. So, she would chat to me from the doorway, with it becoming a standing joke, that the toilet was my office, where we held our meetings.

She always wore bright red lipstick. Tracey is one of the kindest, most compassionate people you could meet. Nothing was too much effort for her and she never let me down during my time in hospital, not only being there for me, but also for my family. I remember one of her first roles in helping me, was to problem-solve the situation regarding the buzzer I had to use to alert staff if I needed help. As my hands were out of commission, I was unable to press the buzzer. Tracey managed to have a door bell rigged up to a blood pressure pump, via a piece of tubing. To get the bell to ring, I had to press the pump with my elbow. It worked and this ingenious invention would remain with me for many weeks to come. It was so vital to me to be able to alert staff when I needed help. It went on to help a woman in another ward who also had mobility issues, and I'm sure it will be used in the future, due to its simple but effective purpose.

*

It was during my stay in HDU that I was introduced to the BLUE CHAIR, which went with me when I left HDU to move to a hospital ward. It had been decided by the team of medical staff who were looking after me, that I needed to be out of the bed and sitting up for a short time each day. So, I would be put in a hoist and lowered into the chair. It felt very uncomfortable, which could have been due to my body feeling sore after being in a coma.

I attended a group called 'INSPIRE', which was created to help people who had been in a coma. The group commenced just as I was discharged from hospital and I attended it for five weeks. One of the things I learned was that whilst being in the coma, I had lost 2% of my muscle mass per day. As I had been in a coma for eight days, I had lost a substantial amount of my muscle mass. This was possibly why my body felt like lead, and I felt weak and unable to move.

Anyway, back to the Blue Chair. I would be left sitting in it for a short time to begin with and I hated it so much. I would be propped up in the chair with pillows for support. It had a footrest, and the staff would put a pillow on it so that I could rest my legs. That didn't make me feel any more comfortable. As I lay in that chair, I would gradually slip down it. I was unable to prevent myself from doing this, no matter how hard I tried. I had no control over my body and I felt really frightened, thinking "What's happening to me?" But I was too scared to ask, as I don't think I really wanted to know. I remember being wheeled over to the window, my sister coming with me. This was to enable me to see the outside world, but I remember being uninterested in anything and just feeling uncomfortable and wanting to be put back in my bed.

Looking back on my time in HDU, I now recognise how scared and vulnerable I felt. I think I was able to cope with the horrific situation I found myself in, by portraying an acceptance of the situation and going through the motions. However, when I was told that I was to be transferred to Ward 33, after my condition was viewed as no longer life-threatening, I panicked. I became frightened at the prospect of going somewhere else, which I now believe was because I was becoming more coherent and alert and so felt more vulnerable. I recognised that by moving to Ward 33 I would no longer have a nurse with me at all times for support and that was really scary. I couldn't do anything for myself so, 'Who would be there, when I was in need of help?' But the staff recognised how scared I was and arranged for two of the staff from Ward 33 to come and talk to me and reassure me that I'd be alright. I would have my own room and staff would be around when needed. They were so nice and understanding and they helped alleviate some of my fears.

CHAPTER 5

Ward 33. The First Few Weeks

Later that day, I was transferred to Ward 33. It was Monday the 19th of March and apart from a couple of admissions to Ninewells Hospital in Dundee, I'd be a patient in the ward until Friday the 24th of August - one day off 6 months in hospital, with a total of 20 weeks and 2 days in Ward 33.

It was early evening and my fears of transferring to the ward were reduced by two of my friends being in my side room, waiting on my arrival. It helped to have Debbie and Tracy there, as I could focus on them, rather than on being somewhere strange and away from my comfort zone, which had become the High Dependency Unit. Months after that visit, Debbie and Tracy would laugh, stating that at first, I'd come across as very lucid, but very quickly became incoherent, talking gibberish, obviously showing the effects of the high number of drugs I was receiving. I remember a student nurse caring for me on arriving at the ward. She knew Debbie through work and it felt good to be talking about their involvement with each other, rather than talking about me.

My boyfriend also visited and I remember feeling a bit awkward as I introduced him to my friends. As our relationship was in the early stages, he had not met many of my friends and family and meeting them in these circumstances wasn't how I imagined their first meeting would be. I also didn't realise that it would be the last time I would see him. I don't blame him for making the decision to walk away, as staying with me would have been a massive commitment. Our relationship was fairly new, so it was really too much for him to commit to. I know myself, if the tables were turned, I would probably have done the same. Perhaps that sounds uncaring, but my first thoughts would have been to prioritise the effects my change of circumstances would have on my family and myself. I know I would want to protect them foremost and that's probably what he did.

If I'm being honest, he would not be the only one disappearing out my life that year and that has been hard to comprehend and deal with. My relationship with some of my family members broke down as a result of them not listening to me but choosing to focus on what they thought my needs were. Tragically, these relations have never recovered. I needed to be strong and determined, to make sure I was listened to, in order to be able to cope with what was happening to me. People needed to understand and accept that the decisions I made, were made in my best interests.

Most of my work colleagues stopped communicating with me early on in my journey, and I am extremely grateful to the ones who stuck by me and still do. Their visits have been so important in keeping me strong and in not letting me worry about why my other colleagues have disappeared from my life.

I contracted sepsis through no fault of my own, but sometimes I feel I'm being punished for this, with me losing so many relationships along the way. This has caused me so much anxiety and stress when I so didn't need it, as the battle I was dealing with as a result of this horrible illness was more than enough for me to contend with.

I'm so thankful that most of my family have been with me every step of the way and its true to say, that my relationships with them and my extended family have become even closer. That has been a positive. My close friends have also been faithfully by my side and even friends that I had lost touch with have come back into my life. My friend Ann, who had been part of the family when I was grown up, is now back in my life and visits me regularly. I realise that taking into account the relationships I have lost; I am still lucky to be surrounded by so many people who are there for me.

I recognise that some people found it too hard to visit me, not able to cope with seeing me without limbs. There were also others who visited me and then didn't visit again. This could have been because they found it too hard seeing me as I now was. I'll never know their reasons, but I've learned to accept it and not dwell on why.

*

Little did I know that my stay in Ward 33 would be a time in my life, that although filled with some horrific memories, would also be a time when I would be cared for by such an amazing staff. They would be there for me every step of the journey that was in front of me, supporting me every step of the way. They would be there to wipe my tears and help me find the strength to keep going. They would encourage me to achieve things I never thought I'd be able to do again. I learned to trust them implicitly and they helped me find me again. I now see every one of them as my friends and I love them with all my heart.

I wasn't aware when I arrived in Ward 33 that the staff hadn't nursed anyone like me before. A patient whose hands and feet were dying and turning black. A patient who was to have quadruple amputations in order to save her life. If I'm honest, I still hadn't acknowledged that myself and I think that was because it was too hard and unimaginable. It was months down the line before I was made aware of how apprehensive they were on my arrival. One nurse told me that she had felt like a rabbit in the headlights, nursing me seemingly daunting.

During my first night in Ward 33, I was cared for by a male nurse. He was so kind to me during that night, alleviating my anxiety and fears of being somewhere new. I was feeling very vulnerable and he chatted to me and tuned in my television to help me pass the time, as I wasn't sleeping well and just dosed on and off during the night. Little did I know when I met him that night that we would get on so well. He will probably never know how much I appreciated how caring he was towards me and how safe he made me feel, particularly in those early days. During my time on the ward, our friendship developed to the point where we would often have long one-to-one conversations, with him being extremely honest with me, which I appreciated. We had a similar sense of humour and we'd have many a laugh, usually at my expense.

As I had little appetite and wasn't eating very much, I was attached to a drip every night and fed through a tube which lead through my nose to my stomach. The drip remained in during the night and was disconnected in the morning, with the tube being attached with micro tape to my right cheek during the day. I remember this procedure as not being one the staff was too familiar with. During the first few days, getting it connected at night and up and running was problematic. On one occasion, I remember tasting the liquid at the back of my throat. It did not taste very pleasant. It turned out that the tube was no longer in my stomach, but at the back of my throat. It was not long after that, that the decision was made to take the tube out, as I was beginning to eat a little more. I also was on oxygen, as my oxygen levels were of concern and this was problematic too, as the tube kept falling out of my nostrils and the staff had to keep reattaching it as I couldn't use my hands to do it myself.

Then of course, there was the medication. I received intravenous medication through a cannula and also oral medication. As these were controlled drugs, two nurses would come into my room with the Controlled Drug Book, ask my name and date of birth, give me my medication, then sign the book, verifying that I had received it. This ritual would take place for many weeks, with nurses knowing my date of birth off by heart, having heard me say it so many times. All these procedures were new experiences for me, and I found it all a bit overwhelming.

I also received a daily Fragmin injection. This was given to prevent me from developing blood clots, due to me being bedridden. Little did I know then, that I'd continue to receive a daily Fragmin injection for the duration of my time in hospital.

Then there was my blood being taken practically every two days, again for most of my time in hospital. Two tubes of blood were collected. One was tested for infection and the other was to check my kidney and liver function because of the trauma these organs had endured when I was battling having contracted sepsis. This procedure would be done by a Phlebotomist Nurse, who, with her colleague, would become well known to me. Even after leaving hospital, they would make a point of coming to talk to me if they saw me whilst in the hospital for physio, as an outpatient.

Whilst I was in hospital, they would pop their heads round my room door every morning and say, "I've got you on my list this morning,

Marguerite". Sometimes they would say that I wasn't on their list, but on most of these occasions, they would then return to inform me, my name had been added. As a result, I soon became unperturbed at having them search for a vein to use to extract blood. I've never had visible veins in my arms and I was often amazed by the skill they showed in finding a vein with so little effort.

By the time I arrived in ward 33, my hands and legs were really beginning to look discoloured. My hands were going black and were surreal looking, particularly as I had shellac purple and silver nail varnish on my finger nails. It had been a monthly routine for me to have my nails done and something that identified me as a person. I miss having my painted nails, just as I do many other things that I am no longer able to achieve. I had slim hands and piano fingers, just like my Dad's, and people often complimented me on my long fingers and painted nails. I remember my friend Debbie laughing whilst visiting me and when I asked her what was so funny, she said it was because, every month in the office, I'd get in a fluster when one of my shellac nails would fall off and here I was lying with my hands dying and all my nails were intact. Reading this, you might not think it funny, but throughout my journey, it was having a sense of humour and being able to laugh at what was happening to me, instead of crying, that helped me cope. A coping mechanism that I still use to enable me to remain positive.

However, as the days went by, my hands and feet became blacker in colour. I didn't like seeing them and didn't want my visitors to see them either, so I had them covered up in bandages. Looking back, I now know that if I hadn't been so unwell, I wouldn't have been able to cope. At the time, I don't think it registered with me that this horrific experience was real and was happening to me. I couldn't have, as I would have been emotionally traumatised and hysterical.

The condition of my legs in particular was monitored daily by doctors and a trip to X-ray took place with Kim and Emma coming with me, to see the extent of the damage that had been done. Dates were made for the amputations to take place. The operation on my hands was set for Tuesday the 3rd of April, and my legs were to be operated on exactly two weeks later, on Tuesday the 17th of April. This was to allow the doctors time to assess at what position my legs should be amputated. They were hoping they could amputate below the knees, as this would be more beneficial to me regarding being able to balance, and so they allowed more time for recovery and healing.

My arms were operated on separately. My left arm was amputated from below the elbow by one surgeon and my right hand was operated on by a Plastic Surgeon. She came to my room to introduce herself to me and requested to meet with my family to explain the procedure that was to take place. She met with Kim, Sean and myself one evening and she explained she was going to try to save as much of my hand as possible, in the hope that I would have some form of function in it. I remember Sean asking her numerous questions regarding the impending operation and he also asked, if in the future, there would be the possibility of me having hand transplants. Although she didn't rule out the possibility, she explained the enormity of this becoming a reality. The process of finding a match, along with my age, meant I could be well into my sixties before a match could be found. She suggested that we should concentrate on saving what she could of my hand. She also advised us to start fundraising, stating that the NHS would provide me with prosthetic legs, but might not provide me with a bionic arm. She explained that I would need significant adaptations done to my home and special equipment would be required as I would be severely disabled.

At the time, I still hadn't recognised or acknowledged what was going to happen to me and when I think of it now, I don't know why I didn't. It wasn't as if both surgeons hadn't explained it to me, but it definitely hadn't sunk in. It couldn't have, or I would have been traumatised and in severe distress, and I wasn't. I seemed to show little emotion or fear of the horrific deformities that were about to be inflicted on me in order to save my life, and just like I'd been in HDU, I seemed to just go through the motions with an acceptance that stopped me facing reality and all that entailed.

The memories I have of the next few weeks are horrific and they will remain with me forever. I know now, looking back, that I showed a strength I never knew I had. How else would I have coped?

On the run up to my amputations, I found it hard being confined to bed. Kerry and Tracey visited me every morning, along with the consultant, to look at my hands and feet and discuss my care. I did listen to them and the feedback they gave me, but to be honest it went right over my head and I didn't retain most of what they told me. I never thought to ask questions.

Kerry and Tracey both worked Monday to Friday. They worked with me on these days, listening to my needs and trying to help me achieve them. I remember my bed faced my toilet and shower room, as the notice on the door told me this. It felt cruel to have me looking at these words all day, knowing that I couldn't access it. I was given bed baths and my hair was at first washed with these horrible shampoo bags that were put over my hair. The staff were so nice and recognised the bags did not make my hair look washed at all. So, they devised a method whereby they pulled me up the bed until my head hung over the end of it, tipped the bed downwards and then washed my hair in a basin of water placed on a chair under my head. It was a bit scary, as I'd no control over my body, couldn't use my hands or feet to hold on with and was scared I'd slip off the bed. But, having my hair washed, did make me feel better.

My continual begging to have a shower, led to Kerry and Tracey arranging for the staff to use a hoist, which was needed to lift me out of my bed and into a shower chair. I hated the hoist. My mum had had to be transferred using this piece of equipment when she was living in a care home and it highlighted so many emotions of loss for me. The loss of my mum, the loss she must have felt of no longer being able to move independently, the loss of her dignity and of course, the loss of my own mobility and dignity. I knew my bottom was exposed when in the hoist, but I chose not to dwell on this, as my main objective was to get in the shower. I was lowered into the shower chair and wheeled into the shower room. There was a mirror in the room and for the first time since arriving in hospital, I could see myself and how I looked. It shocked me. Looking at myself, was like looking at someone I didn't know and that person looked so much older than me. I remember feeling my emotions heighten, but pushing them away, recognising the need to be strong, knowing it was the only way to cope with this nightmare.

Once in the shower, it felt so good and so refreshing. Feeling the water wet my hair and body made me feel clean, for the first time in what felt like forever. However, the memory of that shower will always remain with me, but for other reasons. I remember the nurse hosing my legs with hot water. My legs were going black and had the appearance of having been badly burnt. They were raw and covered in sores and as I watched the water being sprayed on them, I could see the gunge and skin slide off and flow with the water down the shower drain. I remember thinking, "Why am I not in pain, as the water is hot and my legs are raw and sore?" The nurse never lifted her head to look at me, but kept asking me if I was alright or in any pain. Looking back now, I realise that the nurse didn't look up because she was probably upset at the scenario, she found herself in that day. I also now recognise, that the reason that my legs didn't feel sore as the nurse hosed them down, was because they were dead and there was no feeling in them.

Although my legs were dying in front of me, Kerry encouraged me not to cross my legs, as they were trying to save as much of my legs as possible. Crossing my legs could stop the circulation in my limbs. This would add to my problems, and I had enough of them to deal with without adding another one.

As my limbs became blacker, I remember asking for them to be bandaged so that people visiting did not have to witness this horrific sight. My son-in-law Sean visited me on one occasion and joked that visiting me was like being in a scene from the television series, 'Silent Witness' as my limbs looked dead, as though they were part of a corpse.

People have told me that my hands looked like black velvet and as I had purple and silver nail varnish on, they must have looked really freaky. Although I can remember everything that was happening to me at the time, I still cannot visualise how my hands looked. This, I have been told, could be due to my brain protecting me from this memory and that I might remember how they look in time to come, but might not.

*

Kim and Sean brought my granddaughters Erin, aged 6 and Gracie, aged 17 months, to see me. Erin, although she'd had what was happening to me explained to her, would sit in a chair in the corner of my room and stare at me with a look of confusion and fear in her eyes. Goodness knows

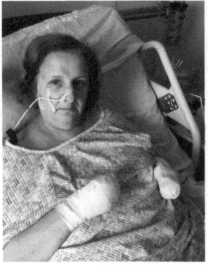

Figure 10;
Me with my feeding tube in & my hands
bandaged

what she must have been thinking. It must have been hard for adults to comprehend what was happening to her Gran, never mind a child. Gracie on the other hand, just took it all in her stride and loved to climb up the sides of my bed. Their visits only lasted 10-15 minutes, as Kim and Sean were frightened Gracie would hurt me unintentionally, as she would want to sit beside me on my bed and give me a cuddle. That wasn't possible as I was in so much pain, but she was too young to understand that.

Emma visited also, but if she didn't appear on a daily basis, I knew it was because she wasn't coping. She was only eighteen and she found me being so ill difficult. She also was living in the house on her own and found it unbearable not having me there. She would try to put on a brave face for me, but I knew she was struggling. Sometimes she just couldn't hide it and would break down in tears.

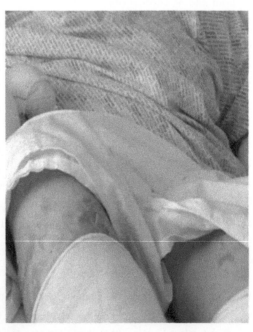

Figure 11; My bandaged legs.

As I had a catheter, I did not need to worry about passing urine, but I still needed to move my bowels naturally. I found using a bed pan really difficult. It is not the natural way to go to the toilet and it was so undignified and uncomfortable to use. My poor diet and fluid intake, as well as the medication I was taking, led to me being unable to move my bowels. I'd never really experienced constipation and I hope I never have to again, as the discomfort became unbearable and found me wriggling in the bed. I was prescribed medication, but it didn't work and eventually I was given an enema. As I found going on the bed pan difficult, the staff would lower me onto a commode. It felt humiliating and even more so, as being unable to use my hands meant the staff had to wipe my bottom for me too. I did learn to accept this, as my dignity had been affected in so many ways and this was just another one of those occasions I had to deal with.

Looking back now, I also know that my lack of appetite didn't help, but I was struggling to eat food, with even my ability to chew proving difficult. I remember being given a chewy fruit sweet by my sister, to try and stimulate my taste buds. But the sweet got lodged in my throat, leading to me choking and being unable to breathe. The sweet was dislodged by banging me on the back, but it was a scary situation at the time. I didn't eat chewy sweets for a long time after that.

As I couldn't use my hands, the staff had to feed me and give me drinks. I recognised that every staff member had a different way of feeding me. For the first few weeks I'd have toast for breakfast. Some staff would put the toast to my mouth, so I had to bite it in the middle. My cheeks got covered in butter, so I had to ask them to wipe it off. Some did not give me enough time to swallow each mouthful, before giving me another bite. The staff were trying their best to assist me and I knew they weren't aware of how difficult it was for me, to feel like I was being fed like a baby. I mostly had soup and yogurt for lunch, as it was easier to be fed with these foods, but not being able to feed myself, affected my appetite and meant I never finished eating anything I was given.

My fluid intake was poor too, as I was receiving drinks in a beaker with a spout and all drinks seemed unpalatable. I remember the beaker bringing back memories of my mum being given drinks in a beaker, whilst residing in the residential care home, as her small motor control and coordination was poor. I recognised that I was being cared for just like my mum was and that scared me. She was 89 years of age when she died and I was only 54 years old, 35 years younger than she was. I remember thinking, "How has my life come to this?"

I was struggling to comprehend what was happening to me, but on the other hand, it didn't feel as if it was happening to me. How could it be? The staff seemed to recognise this and it was then I got my first visit from the hospital Chaplin. I'm not a religious person, but it was good to talk to someone I didn't know, so could be honest in talking about how confused and frightened I was feeling. He would visit me only one other time after that and I don't know why that was.

I had so many visitors over the next few weeks that a rota had to be put in place as I tired easily. I knew many people left my room upset, having seen me for the first time, but they mostly managed to keep control of their emotions until after their visit.

I did appreciate seeing family, friends and colleagues, as I was feeling so isolated. I was unable to use my phone and if I received a text or a call, I could only look at it and see the person's name that had tried to contact me. I felt so useless. The staff would tell me to ring for them and they would answer it for me, but I felt they were busy and answering my phone was not a priority.

I remember a visit from the owners of the residential children's home where I had been working on the day that I noticed the paper cut on my finger. I told them how isolated I felt from the outside world, especially as I was unable to use my phone. The next day, they returned with an ALEXA, that could be linked up to my phone. This enabled me to ask ALEXA to phone anyone I needed to contact. They also brought me a portable TV, an Amazon Fire Stick, a tablet, and iPad, with numerous novels on it and a Pen Drive with lots of movies on it. My big sister was there when they visited and I remember asking her after they left, "Why had they been so generous and kind?" and her saying to me, "Did you not hear what they said to you? They said you deserved these gifts from them and the Meadowview Family, as you were a wonderful person." The staff would visit me on mass a few days later, bearing more gifts. Their generosity was truly humbling and I miss them so much. They were an amazing team to work with and their actions after I became ill, emphasised this tenfold.

As a result of me receiving an ALEXA as a gift, Kerry made it her mission to have it tuned in to the hospital's main wi-fi site, as the patient wi-fi site was not adequate for it to function. Once the IT Department recognised the need for me to be able to communicate with the outside world, this was achieved and ALEXA would function in my room until I was discharged from hospital. I was the first patient in the hospital ever to be allowed to be linked to the main wi-fi system.

Anyway, back to visitors. I began to get inundated with them and so the decision was made to put a cap on how many could visit each day and for how long, as I became too tired to cope with the influx on a daily basis, especially if they stayed too long. I also couldn't cope with visits after 7-7.30 pm and so I requested no visitors after this time. I remember often falling asleep on visitors and I would try hard to keep my eyes open, but couldn't.

My big sister Dianne visited one day, unannounced. She lives in Ayrshire and had only visited me the day before, so her visit was a surprise. She explained that she had to come and let me know about a book event she had attended that morning in Lochwinnoch. She needed to tell me in person, how exciting attending the talk had been, because for the first time since she had been told I was to lose my legs, she had hope that I would walk again. The talk she had attended that day, was by Corrine Hutton, the founder of the charity 'Finding Your Feet', which helps amputees and their families. Corrine had contracted sepsis about five years previously and she too had lost her hands and feet. Dianne explained that Corrine had walked into the hall, without aids and wearing sandals. She was convinced that if Corrine could walk, so could I. Dianne and Trevor had spoken with Corrine and told her my story, which they had found very difficult emotionally. Corrine signed a copy of her book for me, using both her stumps to hold her pen. She told Dianne that she would be happy to come and see me and Dianne was keen for me to do that. However, I wasn't in the zone to speak to anyone about what the future held for me. I didn't want to think of my future, or see someone who had their limbs amputated, as I was scared to even imagine what I'd look like. But I did recognise that I might want to meet with Corrine in the future and therefore told Dianne, that I wasn't willing to meet with her at the moment, but would probably contact her in the future, when I felt ready to do so. Some of my family have read Corrine's book, also called 'Finding Your Feet', with me reading it after I left hospital, when I was emotionally ready to do so. My right hand was also stronger and more functional, so I was more able to turn the pages and keep the book open, using my left arm stump. The book highlighted many similarities with Corrine and myself, but everyone is individual and can't be compared with each other. This has become more apparent, as my journey has progressed.

Get well cards and messages started to arrive. They were not just from family, friends and colleagues, but from so many people from my community, my work community, old workmates and even people I didn't even know. Many of them contained messages of support and encouragement and I couldn't believe the kindness I was experiencing.

Looking back now, I know people would have been shocked when hearing that a small paper cut had caused what was happening to me and wanted to let me know that they cared, as there would have been an awareness that, it could easy have happened to them too.

The fundraising for my needs, once my amputations had taken place, began with my daughter Kim setting up a 'Just Giving' page

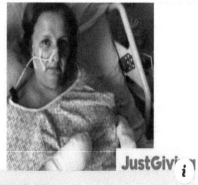

JUSTGIVING.COM
Help raise £80000 to Help Marguerite live again.

Figure 12; The Fundraising page was launched.

on-line. I'd never heard of this method of fundraising before, but Kim had spoken to people who were familiar with it and had been advised, that it was a successful way of raising money. She had written a statement for my page, explaining the background to why the page was being set up, which highlighted sepsis as being the reason for me soon to become a quadruple amputee. I agreed on its content and the use of the photo that was used also. Little did I know what launching my 'Just Giving' page would lead to and the response it had still astounds me and makes me feel so humble.

*

The day after the page was launched, Kim received a phone call from The Sun newspaper, asking if they could do an article about me. My experience had coincided with the government's sepsis campaign, which had been launched just that February. I was aware of this, as I had watched adverts publicising it on my tv, in my hospital room. Kim informed the reporter that she would have to discuss the request with me first. I wasn't sure I wanted to be in a national newspaper, as I'm a private person, who wouldn't choose to be in the limelight. However, I did recognise even then, that telling my story would highlight how serious sepsis is and of the urgency to get medical help to avert serious outcomes. It would also help publicise my fundraising campaign and that could only be beneficial. I recognised too, that I was safe from any publicity the article might bring, as I was in hospital. As I was not well enough to be interviewed, I agreed for Kim to meet with the reporter on my behalf. Kim phoned me after the interview to tell me that she had been asked if there was a picture of me when in the coma (as shown in figure 4). Kim had taken such a picture, as she knew that I would want to be made aware of what had happened to me. I had always been a person who needed to be in control of my own life and would have found it difficult, not to have an understanding of how unwell I'd been. The picture explained all that. That picture was a very personal picture, showing me at my most vulnerable, but I recognised that the article would be much more powerful if it was used and so I agreed for Kim to give it to the reporter. Unfortunately, the article appeared in the press before we could alert all my family and it appearing on the front page of a national newspaper was quite shocking for them to see. It was one of those things that couldn't be helped and was not intended to upset anyone. At the end of the day, if I could cope with a picture of me in a coma being in the newspaper, surely that was the main priority. The success of the article in raising awareness of sepsis and the support it created for my fundraising campaign, proved how powerful the story turned out to be, and that to me made it worthwhile.

CHAPTER 6

Operation Number 1

The day arrived for the operation to remove my left hand and try to save as much as possible of my right hand. You would think that the enormity of what was about to happen to me would have meant that I was in a state of fear and trepidation, but I didn't feel any emotion. The surgeon and the plastic surgeon visited me to explain both procedures and informed me that my operations were scheduled for 2pm that afternoon and would be done simultaneously.

The anaesthetist also came to see me and to be honest, I didn't really understand what he was telling me. He did ask me if there was anything I wanted to say, but I explained that I didn't really know what to expect as the only operation I'd had, was when I'd had my tonsils removed when I was 9 years old. I asked him to make the operation as pain free as possible, as I would have to go through it all again, when my legs were to be amputated in two weeks' time. I did not want to have to worry about another operation looming ahead of me.

I'd been on nil to eat or drink since midnight and spent the morning watching the clock, which was on the wall facing my bed. Time seemed to go so slowly. Kim, Sean and Emma arrived to sit with me and looking back, it's hard to imagine how they were feeling, or how they coped, knowing that in a short time, their mum would be going to theatre, to get her hands amputated. I remember us all trying to keep up beat as the time got nearer to 2pm, but I was becoming agitated and scared and found it hard to keep control of my emotions. Looking back, I recognise

I was panicking about having to have an operation, not because of going to theatre to have my arm and fingers amputated. I think the high dosage of pain killers I had been given, and my brain protecting me from the reality of it all, stopped me from acknowledging how horrific everything really was. Kerry had asked me previously if I would like her to be with me in theatre. By now I had already built up a trusting relationship with her and I knew her presence would be of great support. She arrived to go with me just as the theatre staff arrived to take me down to theatre.

At this point I did begin to panic and couldn't hold back the tears. I remember taking deep breaths to try and keep calm as we entered the lift, with Kim, Sean and Emma standing at one side of my bed. One of my daughters held my hand, but I can't remember who it was. Kerry was at the other side of my bed, holding my left hand and I now realise that that was the last time someone would hold my hand. I would never be able to have my hand held again. I've spoken to Kerry about this and she herself hadn't realised how significant that moment was either. She would as promised, stay in the theatre with me and watch the operations take place. When discussing that day, a year later, on the anniversary of the operation, she told me that she'd recognised that she was witnessing something historical. Two of the finest surgeons in the country were operating on my arms simultaneously. One was a vascular surgeon, amputating my left lower arm and the other was a plastic surgeon, trying to save as much of my right hand as she possibly could.

Anyway, back to being in the lift, on my way to theatre. I was trying hard not to sob uncontrollably, when the theatre nurse, at the bottom of my bed stated, "You need to get a grip!" I can recall trying to compose myself and stop myself from crying. Once back on the ward, Sean broached the subject of the nurse's lack of compassion and of the inappropriateness of her remark, especially as I might never be able to grip anything again. The situation was not only horrific for me, but also very hard on Kim, Sean and Emma. We raised our concerns with the charge nurse, who justifiably brought them to the attention of the theatre staff. They came to the ward to speak to me and apologised for the nurse's lack of empathy and compassion, at a time when I needed support and reassurance.

Anyway, back to what happened next. On arrival at the theatre doors, I had to say goodbye to my family, with it being a struggle for us all trying to be brave for each other. I was then wheeled into a room to be prepped for theatre and slid from my bed, using a slip board, onto the theatre trolley. I had experienced this before, as I had been transferred this way when being taken to x-ray on a couple of occasions and I found it scary as I was frightened, I would fall, due to not being able to use my hands to hold on with.

What happened next will remain a memory I will never forget, as it was so horrific. I woke up after my operation in excruciating pain and thought I had awakened whilst my left arm was still being operated on. I remember screaming for help and wriggling about the bed, as I couldn't cope with the excruciating pain I was feeling. If someone had given me medication to end my life at that point, I would have taken it, as the pain was absolutely unbearable. I remember the nursing staff talking to each other around my bed and trying to calm me down, but the pain seemed to continue forever. Eventually I saw the anaesthetist looking down at me and I could tell that he was alarmed. After being given more medication, eventually the pain diminished and I began to relax. But the experience led to me being taken back to HDU, instead of to Ward 33, so that I could be monitored overnight. My condition had deteriorated.

Early next morning, the male nurse from Ward 33 came to see me, straight from working a nightshift, to make sure I was alright. He will never know how much his visit meant to me. I was feeling so unwell, frightened and confused about what had happened to me and him showing that he cared enough to take the time to come and see me, was so appreciated.

I also had a visit from the anaesthetist, who popped his head around my bedside curtain and asked if it was alright to talk with me. He explained that he had come to apologise to me for the excruciating pain I had experienced the day before, stating that he had not given me the correct dosage of medication to control the pain. Although his confession left me shocked, I accepted his apology, as being angry with him wouldn't change what had happened. However, as my only request to him had been to make the experience as pain free as possible, I was now left even more frightened of what lay ahead for me in two weeks' time.

The next day, I was transferred back to Ward 33, still a bit traumatised. I was continuing to just accept everything that was happening to me without much emotion. My body felt weak and I just felt so tired. Kim, Sean and Emma were waiting for me in my room and they left soon after to let me get some rest.

The plastic surgeon visited me a short time later and requested the bandage be taken off my right hand, to allow her to examine it. I asked for a pillow to be put up as a barrier as I didn't want to see my hand. I've never been the type of person who liked watching surgical programmes on television, or seeing wounds of any type, and I certainly didn't want to look at mine. I also knew I couldn't cope with seeing my hand mutilated and deformed, as I was still not ready to face the reality it would highlight. After the doctor left, pleased with how my hand was looking, the ward charge nurse and the nurse who had taken the bandages off, asked if I wanted to see my hand, saying it didn't look as bad as I was thinking it did. But I knew I wasn't ready to do that. However, I told them Sean would be disappointed in not being there to see it, as he had been so interested in the surgical procedure and had asked the plastic surgeon lots of questions about the operation that was going to be performed. A picture was taken on my phone so that I could show it to Sean when he visited. I would not look at that photo until many weeks later, a long time after even the bandages were taken off.

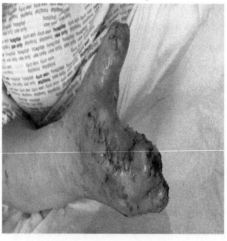

Figure 13;
my right hand, the day after the operation.

On the run up to my impending operation on April the 17th, when my legs were scheduled to be amputated, my health was really poor and I knew that I was still very ill. The visitors kept coming and I know they often left my room in distress. Seeing me with upper limb deformities, even though the bandages hid the reality of how I was going to look physically from now on could not fail to upset them. My legs were looking blacker and more surreal and Kerry would have to keep reminding me not to cross my legs in case I caused more damage to them than there already was. I remember once crossing my legs without thinking, as Kerry walked past the room. But on this occasion, they made a loud, clunking sound, like two bits of wood being hit together, and my heart seemed to stop as I tried to process what I'd just heard. Looking back, I remember that moment being horrific and very scary. On cue, Kerry put her head in my room doorway and told me, 'not to cross my legs too often, as I'd set the bed on fire'. She will never know how effective her words were that day, as instead of becoming upset, I laughed. This was the moment that I realised that my legs were dead and that what I had heard were the bones knocking together. Some people might find that difficult to understand, but Kerry and I had already formed a close relationship and she knew how to work my warped sense of humour, as I hers. During the months to come I relied on getting through the day-to-day challenges I faced with my sense of humour, and the staff were never shy in testing my ability to see the funny side of situations - situations that would otherwise have been too hard to cope with.

I often had a fan on in my room, as my temperature fluctuated and the window would be opened to try and help cool me down. My body also became itchy and caused me a lot of discomfort. I was prescribed antihistamine tablets to try and help ease the constant feeling of wanting to scratch myself all over. This was made even more unbearable as my right hand and left arm were now bandaged and I just had to lie in my bed and wriggle backwards and forwards, to try and become a bit more comfortable. I would watch the clock until it was time to get my next dose of medication. I found it difficult to sleep, so I was awake a lot during the night with the staff often coming in to check on me and on a few occasions they put ice packs under my torso to try and give me relief from feeling constantly itchy.

On a brighter note, Emma passed her driving test and as she already had bought her car, she drove to the hospital to tell me the good news. Passing her test could not have come at a better time for her, as she could now visit me at any time, she wanted to see me and not have to rely on other people bringing her. All the nurses on the ward congratulated her on her news and it was nice to see her smile; she hadn't had much to smile about for some time.

On 9th of April, my condition deteriorated and I found it hard to keep my eyes open. My brother and sister-in-law visited that night, along with my auntie, and I tried so hard to stay awake and talk to them. I could see they were struggling at seeing me so ill and so agitated, as I couldn't lie still. I had a restless night and was given chilled beakers of milk regularly. I'm not a milk drinker, but for some reason, I enjoyed the coolness that drinking the milk brought. My condition was no better in the morning. A staff nurse came into my room and brought a chair over and sat down at the side of my bed. She informed me, that they were concerned about how ill I had become and that the decision had been made to send me, as soon as possible, to Ninewells Hospital in Dundee, where my legs would be amputated, as soon as could be arranged. I began to cry and felt so scared at what was about to happen to me. I also didn't want to leave the security of Ward 33 and the staff I now knew well and fully trusted. The staff nurse told me that she had contacted Kim, who was on her way to the hospital so that she could come with me in the ambulance. I remember lying in my bed watching the staff gathering my belongings together, whilst I tried to control my tears.

The ambulance crew arrived and I began to panic, as there was no sign of Kim. We probably waited only a minute or two before her arrival, but it felt like ages. She arrived with my big brother, who had been visiting me the night before and who was going to follow the ambulance. Once again, the slip board was used to transfer me from my bed to the ambulance trolley and as they wheeled me outside to the ambulance, I felt fresh air on my face for the first time since the 28th of February. The journey to Ninewells seemed to take forever and all I could see was the sky, so I didn't know where I was throughout the whole journey. It was a bumpy ride and I nodded in and out of sleep, with Kim sitting beside me, making sure I was alright. She must have been so worried and scared, but she never showed it. Instead she showed courage and maturity beyond her years.

CHAPTER 7

Ninewells and Operation Number 2

When we arrived at Ninewells, I was taken to this horrible, dingy room, that felt so uninviting. Waiting for me there, were my auntie and uncle, with my big brother arriving a short time later. The doctors arrived and at first, I was told I'd be going down to theatre later on that day, but due to lack of theatre time, it was rescheduled for the next morning.

I was then transferred to Ward 42, with the room being slightly bigger, but not anymore inviting. Then I had nothing else to do but wait. My family visited that evening and as my operation to remove my legs was planned for early the next morning, I told them that there was no need for them to rush back up in the morning, as I was aware it was an hours car journey from home and I didn't want them driving that distance, when I knew they would be in an emotional state. I know I was trying to protect them, but I was also trying to protect myself from getting upset at seeing them upset.

On Thursday the 12th April, I was wheeled down to theatre and was prepped for my scheduled operation. Just as I was about to be taken into the operating theatre, the consultant came to tell me that my daughters had just arrived at the hospital and they were on their way to see me. We all tried to be brave as we hugged and comforted each other, before I told them, that I loved them and that I was going to be alright. Before I was wheeled into theatre, they told me that they'd be there in my room when I returned to the ward.

I awoke in the Recovery Room and felt numb from the neck down. I had no feeling of pain. I remember looking down the bed and all I could see was there was now half of me missing, with what was left of my legs covered in bandages. On the outside of each of my legs were tubes attached to clear plastic bottles, which were circular in shape. I was made aware later that these balls were full of anaesthetic.

It was then that reality hit me. I felt I now looked like a freak of nature and recognised I would never walk on my legs again. Never walk along the beach, feeling the sand between my toes, the sea around my ankles. I would never walk on the grass, feeling it tickle my toes. All the things you take for granted. Then there were my arms, "How could I live without arms?" and "What would I be able to do for myself?"

The enormity of it all overwhelmed me and I sobbed and sobbed and felt I would never be able to stop. 'Why had they saved my life, to be like I was now? ' I couldn't think of any reason why they would want to do that. To me my life was over, as I wasn't ME anymore. My body now looked mutilated, with me lying in a bed, frightened and thinking of what kind of life lay ahead of me.

For the first couple of days I would only let my immediate family visit and I remember trying so hard to be brave in front of them. But sometimes the grief just overwhelmed us all and when they would leave, I succumbed to tears again, as I felt I could no longer be the mum they knew. The mum who had always been there to protect them, to comfort them and make them feel better. I knew they were struggling to be brave and keep strong for me and I felt so guilty, that it was because of what had happened to me, that they were having to cope with this horrific, unimaginable nightmare.

I knew my brothers and sisters were desperate to see me and eventually I felt strong enough to allow them to visit. I remember my older brother and sister-in-law being the first to come and it being a very emotional visit. I'd planned to be strong, more for them than for me, but I couldn't and once the tears started, I couldn't help but tell them how I was feeling and how I didn't want to live anymore. I know they left upset and my brother told me some time later, that he had sobbed once he was out of the hospital, as he couldn't cope with seeing me like I was and he too, didn't know what lay ahead for me. On top of that, he felt he didn't know how he was going to help me.

I remember Emma not coming to visit me for a couple days and I knew it was because she wasn't coping. When she did arrive, she tried to portray a happy appearance, but as soon as I asked her if she was alright, she crumbled. She was struggling with seeing me so ill, but also having to stay in the house on her own. Going home to the house with me not in it, was hard for her. I wasn't there for her to talk to and be the mum she depended on. She had her close friends around her, which I was so glad of, and I knew Kim and Sean were nearby, as was my brother, who lived around the corner from us. They and other family members and my friends supported her in my absence and I so appreciated their help. But it wasn't me, her mum, and I felt so guilty at not being able to tell her that everything was going to be alright, because I knew it wasn't.

On Friday the 12th April, the day after my operation, I was taken by a porter to have a PICC line inserted through my right shoulder. I had no idea what this was and was really scared, as no one had explained the reasons for this procedure. A PICC line is fed through a large vein, that goes nearly to your heart. It allows you to receive medication for a much longer period of time than a cannula. I was so frightened, as I was wheeled into a room, with people all gowned up with their scrubs on, wearing their paper mouth masks. A man explained he was going to insert a PICC line through my arm, using the monitor above, to help him insert it. I remember watching the screen, seeing the line work its way through my body, inside one of my veins. After the procedure was finished, they wheeled me out of the room, into a corridor, telling me a porter would be there soon to take me back to the ward.

On the occasions that I had left the ward at the Victoria Hospital in Kirkcaldy, a member of staff had always been with me, so being in a corridor on my own, in this strange hospital, was unnerving. As I lay there waiting for a porter to arrive, I began to feel I needed the toilet, but how could I be, when I had a catheter in place. As I lay there, I began to feel uncomfortable, as if I was going to burst. There was a clock on the wall facing me and I watched the time extending from one minute to five minutes, then ten minutes. I began to panic and could feel the tears run down each side of my face. People were coming and going around me, but I felt too weak to ask for help. Eventually someone came over to me and asked if I was alright and I explained I was waiting for a porter, but that I had now been lying here for twenty minutes. She went to find out what was happening and came back to tell me a porter would be with me shortly. He arrived five minutes later, with me now feeling in pain and having lain there for twenty-five minutes. When I arrived back in my room, I told a nurse that there was something wrong with my catheter. She examined me and said she could find nothing wrong with it, but I kept insisting there was, as I felt I was going to burst. She eventually noticed that the clip was still on from when it had been emptied that morning, so the urine was not able to escape into the catheter bag, so had been building up in my bladder. That I feel, was the start of my problems throughout my stay in Ninewells, regarding issues with my catheter.

Over the weekend, every time I moved my bowels, I'd pass urine and I felt so degraded. On the day after my operation, I could not move my body to sit on a bed pan, so I had to hang onto the side rail of my hospital bed, with my bandaged arms and move my bowels on a paper mat. The bandages had been removed from my legs to get fresh ones on, so my wounds were exposed during this episode. But nobody seemed to recognise this as inappropriate regarding infection issues, especially as this whole experience was as a result of me contracting sepsis. However, the ritual of me hanging on to the side of the bed continued for the duration of my stay at Ninewells and as I was so ill, I never challenged this. But I felt so humiliated. What was happening to me was unimaginable and I felt so out of control. I seemed to be just accepting everything that came my way, even if deep down, I knew it was wrong.

Anyway, back to the catheter issue. By the Monday evening my catheter was continually overflowing, with a pad having to be placed underneath me, or the bed would have been soaked. I felt so dirty knowing my upper legs were soaked in urine and asked for the catheter to be replaced.

I remember looking at the clock and it was 8pm. The nurse who had agreed to replace my catheter, after examining me, put a fresh pad under me and said she had another task to do, but would be back shortly to replace it. I lay there with my legs open, feeling urine continuously leaking between my legs and as time passed the tears came. The nurse seemed to have forgotten all about me. By 9.25pm, I was distraught, as nobody had come, even after me using all my effort to use the buzzer to summon help. A doctor came into my room and agreed to go and get help. She came back, informing me that it was change-over time for staff, so I would have to wait a few more minutes before a nurse came.

Eventually at 9.50pm, a nurse arrived and informed me that I needed a bigger catheter inserted. I remember thinking that was odd, as the one I had, had worked since I arrived in hospital on the 28th February. But who was I to challenge this, having no nursing experience? A bigger catheter was inserted and as soon as it was, I felt discomfort. I remember asking the nurse if I should feel like this and her saying, it would settle down. I couldn't remember getting the original catheter in, so I accepted what she told me. However, I spent a restless night, as I felt I couldn't close my legs, as I felt as though I had a bag of potatoes inside me. In the morning, I asked a nurse for the catheter to be taken out, as it was too big. She said that the same size of my original catheter had been inserted, but on checking my notes, she saw that I had been correct in telling her that a bigger catheter had been used. She agreed to take it out, only to find that the catheter the previous nurse had used, was not just a bigger size than I needed, but also a male catheter, which is longer. No wonder I was in discomfort. The relief when it was removed was immense.

For the first few days I was given anaesthetic through the balls in my legs and I remember being paranoid about them becoming empty and leaving my wounds without anaesthetic. When they were nearly empty, they were filled only once more and the wait for the anaesthetist to refill them seemed to take forever. I was scared I was going to feel pain, if he didn't arrive in time.

A physiotherapist came to see me, to ask if I wanted physio whilst in Ninewells, but as I had a good relationship with Kerry, I felt it wouldn't be of benefit. I also had no intention of staying in Ninewells any longer than I had to, so it would have been pointless.

During my stay in Ninewells, I asked the consultant every morning to have me transferred back to Kirkcaldy, as I felt so vulnerable and isolated in my room. She would tell me that my condition had to be stable before I could be transported back to Ward 33 and I'd be crying, saying that I would never feel better whilst I remained in Ninewells. My daughter Kim could see how distraught I was and how the issues that I'd faced during my time there, were making me feel vulnerable and frightened. Her concerns led to her visiting Ward 33 without me knowing and asking if they could help get me transferred back there.

The staff were friendly enough, but seemed to always be too busy and in a rush to spend any quality time with me. I had far fewer visitors, due to being much further away from home now, and I felt very lonely. I was extremely weak and I didn't have the strength to request help, so I would just lie there in a room that was uninviting, with no view that would help pass the time. I remember my bed having to be moved quickly one day, away from the wall behind it, as the plugs were sparking. Because it was behind me, I couldn't see what was happening, but knew it was a safety issue. My bed was moved to the far end of my room, below the window, where it remained until I left the hospital, even after an electrician had quickly rectified the problem.

The nursing staff came into my room to turn me regularly in the bed to prevent me from getting bed sores, to give me a bed bath or to feed me, and I hated it. I remember a bank staff nurse, coming into my room to say, she worked at Kirkcaldy and on observing me, asked if I'd had my hair brushed that day. It dawned on me then that I hadn't had it brushed since I'd arrived at the hospital five days earlier, nor had I had my teeth brushed. She also noticed that my medication locker was unlocked. I told her it had never been locked since my arrival. She locked it, but the next nurse who gave me my medication left it open again. My son-in law, Sean, raised my concerns with staff, regarding my hair and teeth not being brushed, as this was a lack of basic care. As for the medication cupboard being left unlocked, he was told, the medication being stored there were not prescribed drugs, so the cupboard could be left unlocked. Yet at Kirkcaldy, all my medication was locked in a medicine cabinet at all times, as standard procedure.

At last, on Tuesday the 17th of April, I was transferred by ambulance back to Ward 33. I was allocated a different room, but it felt as though I was in a five-star hotel, after the dismal room I had in Ninewells. Instead of looking out at a built-up concrete area, I now looked out from above the entrance to the hospital. I overlooked the entrance and the car park, so was be able to watch people coming and going all day long. My Alexa was plugged in and my television also. I really did feel like I had returned home and the staff were so pleased to see me. I remember a nurse who was settling me in, asking what was sellotaped onto my left upper arm and I told her it was my name, as they couldn't put a name band on my wrist. I informed her that when she took it off, my Auschwitz tattooed number would be underneath. I know that sounds bad, but my time at as a patient at Ninewells was not a good experience and it left me quite traumatised and scarred.

I was so relieved to be back in Ward 33. I knew all the staff and I had built good relationships with them. They showed me such care, empathy and understanding. I felt safe.

On the first day back on the ward, I remember a staff member trying to fathom out how to get my pulse, as all four limbs were bandaged and my ear lobes were too small. She eventually got a headband contraption from another ward and once she figured out how it worked, the problem was solved. However, we had a few giggles as other staff members tried to work out how to use it. When it was time for me to move my bowels, I explained to a nurse how I'd been going to the toilet at Ninewells, by hanging on to the side rail of the bed. She was shocked, insisting that I would be using a bed pan in Ward 33. She requested help from another staff member and within less than a minute, I was using a bed pan, getting some of my dignity back.

The next couple of weeks were spent adjusting to living with the limited mobility I had. I had no limbs. I was still very weak and had a catheter in. I still needed to be pulled up the bed using a slip sheet as I had no strength and having no feet or hands, I had no way of pulling myself up the bed. In time, I'd use my elbows to help me achieve this, but that would be once my strength improved. I still had bed baths which I hated, and was still having to use a bed pan. I was aware I was becoming constipated again, so was given medication to help and it tasted disgusting. But I learned that if I drank it quickly using a straw and then drank some juice, it helped. So, I took this medication twice a day, as well as a tablet, to keep my bowels moving. I know I became slightly paranoid about becoming constipated again and would have Weetabix and fresh orange juice for breakfast then prune juice in the evening, all to ensure that my bowels functioned well.

The PICC line that had been inserted whilst at Ninewells was removed. I remember the nurse coming to remove it whilst my brother, sister-in-law and Emma were in the room and they said they'd remain in the room while the procedure took place. The nurse began to pull it out. As we all watched, she pulled and pulled and pulled, removing a line, that seemed to go on for ever. Even the nurse was aghast at how long it was and my family's faces showed how shocked they were. They had not been expecting that to happen! As for me, I just accepted it. After what I'd been through already, I had learned to just accept everything that happened to me, without becoming too anxious or stressed.

The consultant came around every morning and both Kerry and Tracey would be in attendance. They would check my wounds and it wasn't long before the bandages came off my arm and hand, with the wounds having healed really well. This meant I could take a shower, as long as my legs were protected with polythene. I was ecstatic. It also meant that Kim could cut and colour my hair and that made me feel more like myself. She cut it shorter, as we both recognised that I would no longer be able to style my hair, as I had before. She also had to cut it in a style that would cover the bald patch that had developed on the back of my head due to me having been lying in bed for so long. Also, the domestic who came and cleaned my room every day had asked me if I was losing my hair, as there was a lot of hair in the plughole of my shower every morning. I had noticed that there was a lot of hair on my white hospital pillow every morning too and the hair in the plughole just confirmed my fears, that my hair was falling out. I remember jokingly saying to staff that I'd coped with being a quadruple amputee and having to sit in a wheelchair, but, if I had to be a quadruple amputee in a wheelchair with alopecia, I would be throwing in the towel. We laughed about this vision, with laughing and joking being the strategy I used a lot. It was a good coping strategy and as a person, I'd always seen the funny side of things. A good sense of humour was part of my personality, but in reality, it wasn't funny at all, and a bit concerning. However, in time, the condition of my hair improved. Panic over!

I also started to wear my own nightwear, instead of the hospital gowns. As I had a catheter in, wearing pyjamas wasn't appropriate and anyway, all my pyjamas had long trousers, which were no good to me now. I didn't have any suitable nightdresses, so the family was given the task to source some and I ended up with an array of different styles and colours.

My legs were still bandaged, but they did not feel painful, as the drugs I continued to receive kept the pain under control. As the days passed, I began to feel more like myself and as my limbs began to heal, I started to go to the gym with Kerry, so that I could begin to build up my strength. Wearing a nightdress was not appropriate attire for wearing in the gym, so cropped leggings and t-shirts were the next items of clothing to be purchased. The leggings reached to the bottom of my stumps and it did look weird and emphasised that my lower limbs were missing. But wearing clothes made me feel more human and that was a positive thing.

Around this time, I was introduced to a man who had lost his right leg and he began to visit me in my room. We talked about how life was for each of us without limbs and this was so helpful for me. I felt he could relate to how I was feeling, even if not fully. It was the start of a friendship that continues even now. We are a good support to each other, being on the other end of the phone if needed.

CHAPTER 8

My Birthday

The 26th of April was my birthday and the staff came to my room and unwrapped all my lovely presents for me. Tracey sat beside me, opening my cards and reading out the kind words people had written, letting me know I was in their thoughts. I remember Tracey became very emotional as she read them out, with myself and everyone present becoming emotional along with her. The cards were put up on my wall, along with my get-well cards and it was an impressive sight. Many people who passed my room - medical staff, patients and visitors commented on my wall display of cards.

I remember one day, a man and his young daughter stopped at my door. He told me that his daughter had seen the cards and said, "That lady must have lots and lots of friends." She was so right. Seeing all the cards displayed on the wall, did show me how many people cared about me and it did play a big part in helping me to cope with what was happening to me. I often read the messages on them

Figure 14; My impressive wall of cards

Figure 15; My window sill of gifts.

and although they sometimes made me cry, they also gave me the strength to keep fighting.

Anyway, back to my birthday. I spent time in the gym with Kerry that morning, before she and Tracey informed me that they were taking me down to Costa, the café on the ground floor of the hospital. It was situated just inside the main entrance, so I knew there would be lots of people around. I didn't want to go, but Kerry and Tracey were insistent and I eventually gave in and agreed to go, but only if they covered up my amputated limbs with a blanket. I remember feeling really anxious as we arrived at the café. It was the first time I had left the ward without my arms and legs, and in a wheelchair. Tracey asked me where I would like to sit and I told her I would like to sit in the furthest corner of the café, where I could hide and people wouldn't notice me. However, I had only arrived at the table a matter of minutes when two people I knew through work came over to see me, giving me a cuddle and asking how I was doing. They had no idea it was my first time at the café, or how anxious I was feeling. Kerry arrived back at the table with a coffee for me and two cupcakes, which she'd been given by the boy at the counter, after she had told him it was my birthday. Having no hands to hold the cup, I had to drink my coffee with a straw. I was aware of how odd that looked, as I bent over the table to drink each mouthful.

Once back in my room, Kerry asked 'Alexa' to play 'Happy Birthday' by Stevie Wonder and she danced around the room singing along to the song. She kept telling 'Alexa' to turn the volume up, with the song getting louder and louder, and me asking her to turn the volume back down, as she'd get me into trouble. Little did I know that the loudness of the music was to alert the staff that I was back in my room, so they could bring me the birthday cake they had organised for me. They came into my room, proudly holding the cake aloft, with the candles all lit for me to blow out. It was a lovely gesture and so appreciated. It made me recognise more than ever how lucky I was to be in Ward 33, being cared for by the most amazing and caring bunch of staff.

Kim, Sean, Emma, Erin and Gracie visited me that day, with another Birthday cake and presents. My auntie and uncle also visited. It was a quiet day for visitors, which was really unusual, as every other day I'd been inundated with people coming to see me. I think people felt they would give me time with my family, but if I'm honest, it felt weird and more company would have been nice.

Looking back and reflecting on that day, I realise that it was a day full of love, which was clearly shown by the number of cards and gifts I received and by the staff looking after me the way they did. They made my birthday special for me, at a time when I was facing so many challenges and trying to make sense of who I was. I will also remember it, for being the first day I faced the world outside the ward without my legs and arms and how scared I was and also the day I recognised that I'd have to get used to being stared at when in public, due to how I now looked.

CHAPTER 9

The Beginning of My Life Without Limbs

My body was becoming stronger, but getting up from a lying down position first thing in the morning, was hard and still is. I had a special electric bed that made noises frequently, but I got used to that. The bed moved in tune with my body and this prevented me from getting bed sores.

Even though my left hand had been amputated, I felt as though I could still feel my hand and could open and close my fingers. This is still the case, with the constant feeling of pins and needles always being present. I can also still feel my lower limbs and feet and for the first few weeks, after they were amputated, when I was sitting up in the bed, I could feel them going straight through the mattress and dangling underneath. It felt quite surreal.

My sleep pattern was poor and still is, but a contributing factor then was the heat. The weather was hot and continued to be until I left hospital. It meant my curtains and window remained open during the night, so the room was never really dark. Nowadays, I can sleep without my bedroom being dark, as I'm so used to it.

Having no lower legs meant that the bottom of my bed was empty. I remember my sister coming to visit me on one occasion and putting her bags on the bottom of my bed. I commented that it was a bonus me not having legs, as it meant there was space for her to put her bags there. I was joking of course, focussing on seeing the funny side of the situation, but I don't think she did.

I became adept at wriggling up and down the bed. I learned to wriggle backwards onto the commode chair I'd been given. The bed would be lowered to the same level as my chair, enabling me to transfer between my bed and my chair easily. Going into the shower became a much more pleasurable experience, especially when compared with the days when I relied on the hoist. I also began to use a chair called a freeway when going to the toilet to move my bowels. The chair could be pushed over the toilet seat. This meant I no longer needed to use a bed pan and although I still needed help to clean myself, it made me feel more independent. I requested that my catheter be removed too, as there was no longer a need for me to have one as I was able to access the toilet. The minute it was removed, I felt cleaner and less ashamed. I'd hated people seeing the catheter bag lying on my bed, even though I'd try to hide it under my bedsheets when people came to visit me. If I had my leggings on, it would be strapped around my right leg, but it was still visible. Having it removed made me feel a lot more relaxed.

I don't think I'll ever get used to needing help with my personal care, but in the early days, I found it even harder and would often cry when I was on my own, knowing that I would no longer be able to do everyday tasks independantly. The staff were so empathetic and understanding of how degraded and embarrassed I felt and I know they tried their best to reassure me. They constantly told me to ask for help when I needed it, but I knew how busy they were and wouldn't unless I really had to.

I was given my own wheelchair. Like with the freeway chair, I wriggled backwards onto it from my bed. Kerry came and took me to the gym in my chair every morning and we worked on strengthening my core muscles and balance. These were the two main elements I would need to balance on prosthetic legs. At the time it was hard to contemplate how I could possibly even balance on artificial legs, never mind walk on them.

By this time, I had built up a very strong relationship with Kerry and trusted her immensely. She was a good listener and I spoke openly to her about how I was feeling and my fears about finding myself in this surreal, scary life without limbs.

After physio each day, she wheeled me back to my room, where usually some of my family or friends would be waiting with my lunch. I was not keen on the hospital food and eating was still problematic. My family and friends organised a rota to make sure I had food at lunch and dinner time. The staff were always putting food in the fridge for me, so that I was never without tasty food I could eat.

The nutritionist kept a watch on my diet and encouraged me to eat more, as my poor appetite meant I was not eating enough protein in particular. At one point she suggested I have a sausage on a roll for my breakfast. I did try this, but found eating this at quarter to eight in the morning was too much for me. I was never one for eating much for breakfast and this on top of my poor appetite, made eating it unappealing. I was given protein drinks, which tasted horrible and made me feel squeamish. I got Kim to pour them down the sink, which she was not keen to do, but I would plead with her to do as I asked, so that I could avoid drinking them. Eventually I confessed to the nutritionist and it was agreed that the protein drinks would stop. Instead I drank five cups of full fat milk daily, to compensate for the protein drinks. As I had been drinking milk regularly, it seemed a more doable plan. Further down the line, the nutritionist would advise me to stop drinking so much milk as my weight was increasing.

The staff continued to feed me my food, as although the bandages were off my hand and the stitches had been removed, it was still healing and needed to be kept clean. But I wanted to be more independent and be able to feed myself. I practised holding a spoon and fork, and through sheer determination and will power, I quickly managed to use them to enable me to feed myself. However, my independence didn't last long, as one day, when Emma was visiting, I put my hand on my bed trolley and heard a clunk. On inspection, it turned out that a bone was protruding from my half thumb and the stump where my pinkie had been. Operation number 3 was required to cut the bones and re-stitch the wounds.

CHAPTER 10

Operation Number 3

The day of the operation began at 6am. The nightshift staff got me in the shower and dressed me. The male nurse I had got to know so well, was given the task of getting me dressed. But when it came to putting my bra on, he couldn't get it fastened and ended up saying, "Marguerite, I can't put bras on. I can only take them off!". We both laughed and he then went off to find someone who could finish the task of dressing me. I, and the nurse that finished dressing me, often joked with him about what happened that morning, as it was funny. Some people reading this might think how embarrassed I must have been, having a male nurse put me in the shower and dress me, but I'd got beyond being embarrassed. He was a nurse doing his job and I trusted him. I knew he always had my best interests as his priority and what more could I ask for?

The operation on my hand took place at the Queen Margaret Hospital in Dunfermline, so I needed to be transported there by ambulance. As before, I was nil by mouth from midnight and would not receive breakfast. After I was made ready for the journey by the night shift staff, the ambulance crew arrived to pick me up just after 8am.

I will never forget that journey to Dunfermline. I was in my wheelchair, which at that time I could only manage to sit in for short periods of time. I became sore as we made our way there, I could feel myself slipping down the chair. Every time the ambulance went over a bump, I felt myself move further towards the edge of my chair and by the time I arrived at the Queen Margaret, it felt like my seat belt was the only thing keeping me from slipping onto the floor.

Once in the ward, I was left by the side of a bed in a four-bay room. The plastic surgeon came to see me and said she hadn't expected me to arrive until the afternoon, as my operation was scheduled for then. I knew then that it was going to be a long day. Looking back, I never felt scared about going back to theatre. Maybe it was because I knew it couldn't be as bad as what I'd already been through, or maybe because I had learned to just take what was coming in an accepting and unemotional way.

As I said earlier, I could not sit in my wheelchair for too long, as I became sore, but that day, I had to remain in my chair until they came to take me to theatre in the afternoon. I don't know how I coped, as I felt sore and uncomfortable. I remember asking if I could lie on the bed, but was told just to sit in my chair. Maybe if I had explained how I was feeling, the nurse might have let me use the bed, but I didn't have the strength to challenge her, so I continued to sit there. I nodded off at times, unable to keep my eyes open. I had my mobile phone with me and I was beginning to be able to answer it or send texts by holding the stylus between my teeth and I used it to text Kim and Emma and tell them what was happening.

Eventually theatre staff arrived with the trolley to take me to theatre. But there was a problem. How was I to get from my wheelchair onto the trolley? I had no legs to achieve that myself. The ward did not have a hoist, so someone was sent to get one from another ward. The hoist that arrived looked antiquated and it took the staff a minute or two to work out how to use it. Then it was time for me to be hoisted onto the trolley. As I was lifted off my chair, I disappeared inside what seemed like a big bag and I couldn't see anything. It was so frightening. It did do the trick though and I was finally lowered onto the trolley, but when the hoist was removed, I could see the other patients in the bay all looking at me. I felt humiliated. That day was another reminder that I would always be stared at because of how I now looked and how disabled I now was. It was very, very upsetting for me.

I woke up in the recovery room, with my hand bandaged and felt that I was back to square one, having only just begun to be able to use my hand again. I was taken back to the four-bay room and again I was put in the hoist, this time to lower me back into my wheelchair. I would have benefitted from going into the bed, as I felt exhausted. I had been awake since 6am that morning and it was now 4pm in the afternoon. But I was put in the wheelchair, groggy and not having the energy to challenge this decision. I was given a slice of toast and a beaker of coffee. My hand being bandaged meant I couldn't hold a mug or the toast and I needed help to eat it. Then, I waited to be told I could go back to Ward 33. I remember communicating with my sister by text, as she was to visit me that night and bring in my dinner and I let her know I was still at the Queen Margaret. Eventually, the ambulance arrived to take me back to the Victoria Hospital and I arrived back in Ward 33 at around 7pm that evening. I don't remember the journey back, but I remember being absolutely exhausted on my return. My sister had been and gone and had left me something to eat with the ward staff. I did attempt to eat it, but all I could think of was getting into my bed and lying down. I had spent most of the day sitting in my wheelchair and I felt sore and fatigued, finding it hard to keep my eyes open. The same night shift staff that had got me ready to go to The Queen Margaret, were again on duty and got me ready for bed and I remember being so happy to get into bed for the night and go to sleep. I don't remember being in any pain from the operation, only the feeling of being totally exhausted and sore from sitting in my wheelchair for so long.

My fingers healed relatively quickly, with the stitches being removed after a week or so. It only hindered me using my hand for a short time and then it was back to practising being able to hold a fork and spoon again. My hand was very sensitive and weak, so I was only able to use it for minimal periods of time, but even using it for a short time, meant I was building up its strength and function. I now drank from a straw independently, rather than from a beaker, which I'd needed help with. My skills were gradually increasing.

Although there were still dressings on my thumb and pinkie, my hand became more functional once the stitches were removed, and by the end of May, I was able to hold a pen to tick the boxes on my daily menu cards. I also got better at using my mobile, no longer needing to hold

Figure 16; Using a pen to fill in my hospital menu.

the stylus between my teeth, but in my hand.

My thumb healed quickly, with the dressing no longer required. However, it took a few weeks for my pinkie to heal as the dressing was easily knocked off because of where it was. Consequently, I would then knock the scab off my wound. So, as you can imagine, it affected the healing process.

CHAPTER 11

May, An Emotional Month.

After my operation, I quickly returned to my daily physio sessions with Kerry in the gym. My wounds were healing well and the bandages were removed and replaced with dressings. I began to be self-conscious of the hair growing on my legs, but I wasn't allowed to remove it until my scars had completely healed. I couldn't wait for that day to come.

I had been given Juzo stockings to put over my legs. These are compression stockings and are used to help reduce swelling. A consequence of having legs amputated is that the tissue swells, causing them to look bulbous. Wearing the Juzo stockings helps to slowly reduce the swelling. I wore them 24 hours a day. They were hard to put on, as they were very tight fitting, but they did work. I wore them all the time until I got my prosthetic legs. Then I wore them during the night, whilst in bed, when my legs were taken off.

It was around this time that I began to feel pain in my left upper arm when I tried to move it. Applying deodorant became painful when I tried to raise my arm. Kerry gave me exercises to try and help alleviate the pain and put strapping on it to see if that would help. I used to tell people it was my sports injury, if they asked what the strapping was for.

The reality of now having no legs was hitting home. I could not get out of the bed on my own, so unless items were on my bedside trolley, I could not reach them. At the time, I never thought that would ever change. If something fell on the floor, I couldn't get to it to pick it up and as I often dropped my stylus when trying to text, this became very frustrating for me. Tracey came up with the idea of using a wooden rod with a magnet on the end of it and having another magnet attached to my stylus. Although it felt heavy for me to hold at the time, it did work and gave me the ability to do something else for myself.

The recognition that I could hardly do anything for myself began to sink in big time, and although to the world I seemed to be coping remarkably well, inside I was struggling more than anyone will ever know. How was I going to cope when I got home? Even when I eventually got prosthetic legs, they needed to come off at night and then I'd be trapped in my bed. I felt so, so vulnerable and scared and I did cry most nights, but at a time when I was on my own and no one would see me.

I didn't realise that Kim and Sean were also aware of this and they came in one evening and spoke about their fears. They worried about me living on my own when I got out of hospital, and in the future, especially if Emma ever decided to move out of the family home. They explained that they had done a lot of thinking and felt that the best option for me was to have a self-contained annex built onto their bungalow. It would provide me with a home specifically for my needs and encourage me to be as independent as possible, whilst having them next door if I needed their support. At first, I was not in favour of this idea. I had just finished renovating my home and wanted to leave hospital and go home to my own house. But as the days passed, I realised my home was not going to be adequate to cope with my now complex needs and the rooms were certainly not big enough to accommodate my wheelchair. Even though I was beginning to recognise how disabled I was, looking back, I had no idea what my needs would be. But I knew my future, and my home, were not going to be what I'd planned for myself, and facing up to that was not easy.

The 'Just Giving' page launched by Kim in March was a great success. Many of my family, friends, people in my community, people who knew me through work, people from abroad, and many people who just wanted to help, gave generously and the total just kept rising. A couple who knew my twin brother donated £10,000, an incredible amount of money. Kim visited me on a daily basis, and informed me of many fundraising events that were planned - Charity Shows, Music Events,

Sponsored Walks, Half Marathons, Clairvoyant/Spiritual Nights, T-Shirt sales to name but a few. The response from my community was phenomenal and very humbling. Although I recognised that the support was not just because people wanted to help, but also due to the severity of my injuries, I tried not to dwell on that, as it was too upsetting for me to cope with. I just focussed on the fact that people wanted to help me and I really appreciated their kindness and generosity.

The press also continued to show an interest in me and The Sunday Post and The Sun came to the hospital to interview me. They had to put in a request by contacting the hospital and asking for permission. The hospital verified with me that I was okay to meet with them. I found going public quite challenging, but the articles in the paper were a good way of highlighting sepsis. They also provided me with the opportunity to publicise how I was doing to the people who had donated so generously to my fundraising campaign. I felt that was the least I could do.

It was recognised that getting out of the ward was an essential part of my rehabilitation. So, Kerry and Tracey introduced me to a piece of equipment called the 'Banana Board'. This was used to help me transfer back and forth, from my wheelchair to a car seat or toilet seat. The Banana Board is made of hard plastic, was bright yellow, and shaped like a banana, hence its name. Learning how to use it enabled me to leave the hospital during the day, with family and friends.

Tracey arranged with Kim to park her car at the back of the hospital and I was taken down there to practise using the board to get into Kim's car. Tracey explained that the Banana Board was not usually used for people with both legs amputated, but due to how good my balance was, she felt I could use it safely. I achieved using this piece of equipment with minimal practice. Once I was competent, Tracey encouraged Kim and I to go off in the car and enjoy some time away from the hospital. It was one of many memorable moments on my journey and it felt so good to be sitting in the passenger seat of a car, looking like any normal person. Up until then, I had only sat in my wheelchair or freeway chair, which were both disabled pieces of equipment. When in the car, no one looking at me could tell I was a quadruple amputee and that felt good.

We decided to visit my work that day. I knew I would be able to access the building as there was a ramp leading to the entrance door. Going home, or to the houses of any relatives or friends, was out of the question, as they all had steps. My colleagues seemed pleased to see me, but I could tell that for the those who hadn't visited me in hospital, seeing me without limbs was a shock. The conversation was a bit awkward at times, with people watching what they said and trying hard not to mention anything to do with how I now looked. In other words, 'trying not to put their foot in it'.

That day was the start of me being able to get out of the ward on a regular basis and for the remainder of my stay in hospital, I was out and about regularly, often for lunch or tea. I will always remember the first time I went to a restaurant. My sister and brother-in-law, Dianne and Trevor took me, with me feeling very anxious about entering the restaurant with how I now looked. I had Balmoral Chicken, which I needed cut up to be able to eat it, but it was delicious. I remember phoning Kim and my Auntie Teresa and Uncle Joe, to tell them that I was out having something to eat, as id accomplished another milestone on my road to recovery.

I came to know all of the eating places in the area that I could access with my wheelchair. I remember a funny occasion when my auntie and uncle came to the hospital to take me out. After transferring into the car using the banana board, we headed off, only to be alerted by a clattering noise as we drove around the roundabout at the entrance to the hospital. It turned out that my uncle had left the banana board on the roof of his car and it had slipped off, landing on the roundabout. He still gets teased about that yet.

Going out, however, also highlighted how many places I couldn't access and how many barriers there are for disabled people to tackle. Dropped kerbs were not always available, or drivers had parked over them. Disabled toilets didn't have disabled toilets in them, making them too low for me to use, even using the Banana Board. Aisles in shops weren't wide enough to accommodate my wheelchair.

Going out also meant I had to face people looking at me wherever I went and that, I found really hard. Sometimes the person pushing me in the wheelchair had to pull me backwards to enable them to get over door rims. It left me facing groups of people, all watching me in my wheelchair. I hated feeling self-conscious of how they saw me. However, I knew I either learned to cope with the stares or remain in the hospital, isolated from the outside world. I couldn't allow myself to give in.

At the beginning of May, my Mum's brother, my Uncle Tommy, was admitted to Ward 23. I visited him every day. Ward 33 staff would take me down to his room and come back for me if no family members were around to escort me back to the ward. I feel really privileged and so happy to have spent quality time with my uncle over the next three weeks that followed, often being with him on my own. I have precious memories of my time with him that will remain with me forever. He died in hospital on the 19th of May. He was very ill during his time in hospital, but he was always more concerned about how I was feeling, just as he was when I developed sepsis. He and my Auntie Nan were regular visitors until he wasn't well enough to leave the house.

Whilst he was in hospital, if I hadn't visited him at my regular times, he would ask where I'd been and was always pleased to see me. I remember visiting one day and he looked so unwell, but he still displayed his amazing sense of humour. He explained to me that his temperature had dropped during the night and all the emergency services had arrived to help and had wrapped him up in tin foil, stating, ' I felt like one of your Auntie Nan's gammon joints, in the oven'. He was such an irreplaceable character, who was loved by everyone who knew him. He enjoyed nothing better than being surrounded by his family and took great pleasure in teasing us all, having a good laugh into the bargain.

I remember visiting him with Kim and Sean the night before he died. His sense of humour still shone through. He jokingly asked Sean to cut the bottom off the bed, as he kept slipping down it and felt that his feet were being squashed. Of course, Sean couldn't do that, but he did help him move back up the bed and made him more comfortable. He died the next evening, five minutes after I had left him to go back to Ward 33, with his own family around him, which was just as it should have been.

I was able to attend his funeral, which I'm so grateful for. I can't deny it was a difficult thing to do for lots of reasons. I knew I would attract attention and I so didn't want that to happen. It was my Uncle Tommy's day and I wanted it to be about him - a day to celebrate the life of the amazing man that I was privileged to call my Uncle. I sat in my wheelchair at the end of the aisle in the Crematorium, away from most of the congregation, listening to my cousin, Jim, deliver the eulogy. I was so humbled when Jim mentioned my time with his dad before he died. He thanked me for being there for him. I didn't need thanked; I was the privileged one, to have spent special moments with a lovely man. He also stated that the collection for his dad at the end of the service would be given to me, towards my fundraising campaign. What an amazing gesture and truly appreciated.

My mum's friend Margaret also died that month and her family also donated the collection to my fundraising campaign. These gestures from families who were grieving, made me feel so humbled. I knew there were so many other worthy causes that they could have chosen to receive their donations.

My right hand healed well and became stronger, with me challenging myself to do more and more tasks without help. I was given an electric toothbrush by my family as an Easter present. I was able to hold my electric toothbrush on my own, as long as the staff pressed the button to put it on and off and put the toothpaste on for me too. These were tasks that I would achieve later, when my hand became stronger and not so sensitive. I could now also hold my hairbrush and brush my hair independently.

I still had dressings on my hand and they had to be changed after my morning shower, as they got wet from the scrunchy which I could now hold to partially wash myself. The, dressings were also changed often during the day, as they became grubby.

I could now also hold a sandwich, although it depended what the filling was, as anything chopped up, would fall out, leaving me with just the bread. If I had some crisps, the packet would have to be opened for me and then the crisps were put on my plate, as having no fingers, meant I couldn't take them out of the packet. I remember trying to open a family packet of crisps one day, by squeezing the bag between my knees. It didn't work as planned. The bag burst open at the bottom and the contents fell all over the floor. As for biscuits and chocolates, I couldn't open the packaging, never mind remove them from their individual moulds. I tended to give a lot of the chocolates I received from visitors to the staff, after eating only a few. I was aware, being immobile, I wasn't burning up the calories and I couldn't afford to put on weight. The thought of being an obese quadruple amputee in a wheelchair, wasn't a good image of who I wanted to be.

I was now also able to hold a plastic mug for a short time, as it was of light weight. Having no fingers, holding a glass was a task I would never be able to achieve, so drinking juice or milk needed to be with the use of a straw.

I learned to hold a pencil and began to fill in my own hospital menus, instead of the staff doing this for me. The press captured this task and it appeared in the newspapers. To be honest, I knew it would be a while before I could write my name or any word, but I was determined that that would come in time.

Even with now being able to achieve some tasks on my own, my skills were very limited, with the staff having to do so much for me. I needed to be transported to the toilet, with staff cleaning me afterwards. If I was in my wheelchair, I had to wriggle back onto the bed and then wriggle on to the freeway chair, before being wheeled into the toilet. The whole process was repeated in reverse if I needed to go back into my wheelchair. The staff used to joke at how skilful I became at this task. You've no idea how much energy it needed for me to wriggle up and down the bed. There was lots of hilarity when staff tried to remove my pants and leggings whilst seated on the freeway chair and then put them back on again. The amount of ripped pants and leggings that had to be bucketed was incredible.

I still couldn't put any of my own clothes on and again the effort I used rocking backwards and forwards to get dressed in the morning was hard work. I began to realise that wearing bigger sized clothes helped. I remember the hilarity when Emma purchased some bigger pants for me. She had bought them from a well-known store for £3.50 for six pairs. They seemed alright when I first put them on. However, as the day passed, they stretched a little more every time I went to the toilet and eventually, they fell off as I wriggled on and off the bed. I called them my disposable pants, as they went in the bucket at the end of each day.

Every member of staff on Ward 33 showed me so much support and encouragement as I tried to gain more control in regards to being independent. If I achieved a new skill, by the end of the day, all the staff would know about it and would pop into my room to congratulate me. Mind you, they were also awfully good at unintentionally using phrases that mentioned, legs, feet, hands and fingers. It seemed to become a daily event and although at first, they worried about upsetting me, they soon recognised that I had a warped sense of humour and so would laugh when they yet again 'PUT THEIR FOOT IN IT', pardon the pun. You have no idea how many phrases there are related to this topic - 'Stand on your own two feet', 'I'll cross my fingers for you', 'High five' and 'Do you need a hand?' to name but a few. I remember one day a member of staff gave me a friendly telling off, for not wetting my hands before apply the liquid soap and asked me to read the washing your hands poster above the sink in my room, which also displayed pictorial images of each process. As she left the room, I called her back to tell her that I couldn't do it, as the pictures showed two hands and I had only one. We both laughed, as it was funny, even though in reality it was true and highlighted, that even the simple process of washing my hands would have to be done differently. I now had to wash my hand by using my stump also.

I arranged for Corrine Hutton and a colleague from her charity 'Finding Your Feet' to visit me. As I'd mentioned earlier, Corrine had lost her limbs to sepsis a few years previously and I now felt ready to meet her, along with Kim. She arrived carrying a Costa coffee for me and walked into my room, without the use of any aids. To be honest, you would not have known she was walking on two prosthetic legs. Talking to someone who had been through a similar experience to myself and could relate to how I was feeling, was really helpful. She gave me a lot of advice and suggestions that could be of help to me on my journey of recovery. Even her ability to walk so confidently gave me hope that I also would walk again. Her visit was a great boost for me. Corrine left me a gift of a one-legged teddy bear, wearing a 'Finding Your Feet' t-shirt. It sat on the unit in my room for the remainder of my time in hospital.

The fundraising continued to escalate, with many events taking place. Erin's dance school arranged a Charity Show in the Lochgelly Centre on the 27th of May and asked me to let them know my favourite ballad so that Erin could dance to it at the beginning of the show. I found it hard to choose one, as I had so many favourite songs. When my friend and her husband came to visit me, I told them about my dilemma. A few songs were debated and then her husband suggested 'Careless Whisper,' by George Michael. He was mortified when I reminded him that the lyrics were, 'I'm never going to dance again.' My friend and I couldn't stop laughing, but her poor husband took a while to see the funny side of the situation, as he was worried that he'd upset me. He hadn't and to be honest, if I had to get upset about every scenario that highlighted my loss of limbs, I wouldn't have been able to cope. I didn't and still don't want people to walk on egg shells when around me. I just want to be me, the person I was before sepsis struck.

Anyway, I eventually chose the song, 'Immortality' by Celine Dion. It's a song that reminds me of my dad and the lyrics are beautiful.

I attended the Charity Show, sneaking into the theatre just before it started. All my friends and family were already seated there, supporting the event, as well as my attendance at something so public for the first time. Erin opened the show dancing to 'Immortality', which was sung beautifully by Elaine Greene, a singer who had come out of retirement to perform for me. It was a very emotional moment for me to see my granddaughter dance to a song that meant so much to me. Realising that all these children and young people had practised so hard to put on such an amazing show just for me and that there was a packed theatre of people there to support the event, was very humbling. The song danced by the whole cast at the finale was 'THIS IS ME' from the film, 'The Greatest Showman' with the words of the song, so appropriately summing up, the person I'd become. A song that will remain close to my heart. I often become emotional when I hear it, as it takes me back to the Charity Show and how I was then, and I remember the overwhelming emotions and feelings I felt at the time.

During the show I realised for the first time that I could no longer clap. I told Erin how wonderful she had been on the stage and how proud I was that she had danced on her own for her gran, but apologised that I couldn't clap. She just said, 'Gran, just clap with your hand and your stump' and showed me how I should do it. It was clear Erin had adapted well to seeing me with my amputations and was no longer fazed by how I looked.

After the show, my friends took me back to the hospital, where I found myself locked out, as the hospital doors are locked to the public at 10pm. We had to ask at the reception at Accident & Emergency to be let in, which my friends and I found so funny. It's not an everyday event, to be locked out of the hospital where you are a patient, but it wouldn't be the only time it happened to me.

Although the Charity Show was the first big public event I'd attended, I had attended a sponsored walk organised by my friend Helen, at Lochore Country Park just a few days before. It was a beautiful sunny day and although I didn't take part in the walk, I joined in at a picnic afterwards. As it consisted of mainly family, friends and neighbours, I felt more comfortable there. After the event, I visited a friend's garden for a barbecue. I was beginning to have more contact with the outside world.

May was also the month that Kim took me to an appointment at The Astley Ainslie Hospital in Edinburgh to be assessed for an electric wheelchair. Their recommendation was that I required an extending chair which could be elevated to allow me to access places or items which were out of my reach. However, I was informed that the NHS did not provide them and I would therefore receive a normal electric wheelchair. This was the first barrier I'd encountered as a disabled person, but it would not be the last. There would be many, each of them causing me frustration and anxiety.

The Social Work Department was notified, as I would need their involvement throughout my life from now on. This was hard for me to acknowledge, never mind accept. As I mentioned earlier, I knew my house was no longer suitable for my needs and so Tracey arranged for Kim, Sean and her to meet with Social Work at my house and start the ball rolling regarding where I was going to live when I left hospital.

Eventually, the scars on my stumps healed and I was allowed to remove the hair from my legs and even though half my legs were missing, it did make me feel less self-conscious of how I looked. I was now ready to try out Pamm Aids, which were blow up tubes, similar to swimming armbands. A tube was placed over each of my stumps. A metal frame with a foot rocker was placed over the tubes, then they were blown up to a certain pressure. I was then helped to my feet by Kerry, Tracy and another physio. I walked for the first time without my own legs, using

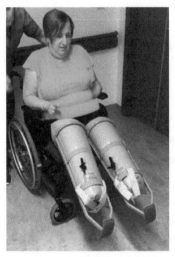

Figure 17:
Me wearing PAMM AIDS

a gutter frame for support on the 31st of May. Kim and Emma were there to witness this very emotional and memorable moment. They captured it on video and shared it with my gobsmacked family. It felt strange to be standing again. I resembled the Marshmallow Man from the Ghostbuster movie. I couldn't bend my knees and walked just like he did in the film. But I was at last standing again and was a step nearer to being able to walk with prosthetic legs. I practised walking wearing the Pamm Aids for a few days, with some of my family and the staff from Ward 33 coming into the gym to see me. There were a few tears shed at the sight of me standing, particularly for the staff, who had never seen me standing before. The downside was that it was now time for me to go back to Ninewells, to be fitted with prosthetic legs and to learn to walk in them. Kerry had told me previously, when we'd talked about this day, that I'd have to stay in Ninewells until I'd learned to walk, and I cried at the prospect of going back to the hospital that evoked so many bad memories for me. Kerry reassured me that my experience this time would be more positive, as I was going to learn to walk.

CHAPTER 12

The Month of June and Back to Ninewells

At the beginning of June, Kim took me to Ninewells to have my stumps cast, the first process in making prosthetic legs. The casts were an accurate way of ensuring an exact fit. The legs were to be made and ready for me when I returned to Ninewells to begin learning to walk again. Rubber socks called 'Icerosses' were placed on both stumps, then wrapped in clingfilm. Moulds were taken, using plaster of Paris, before being left to harden. The moulds were then slipped off, the cling film enabling this process to be achieved. These moulds would form the shape for my prosthetic legs.

Kim, Sean and I had arranged to meet with Social Work when we arrived back home following the appointment at Ninewells. Driving into the village where I lived was very emotional this time, as I seemed to be even more aware of what I'd lost. I passed shops that I used to be able to just jump out my car and pop into for bits and pieces on a daily basis. It was hard for me and I couldn't help wondering how this whole surreal situation had happened. Arriving in the street where I lived, reality hit home. I couldn't help but remember, that the last time I'd driven into my street, I had my limbs and I had been driving the car myself, when driving home from work that Monday night in February. The reality that I would never drive home from work again, or drive anywhere again, was hard to accept. It's hard to describe how weird I felt. It was like this whole thing was a dream and that I'd wake up and be back in time, when I was Marguerite with legs and arms. I felt my heart pound, as I felt sheer panic. The reality of it all hit me like a brick.

Social Work assessed my home and looked at the plans for the extension on Sean and Kim's house. The conclusion was that my own house could no longer accommodate my needs. An annex built onto Kim and Sean's house, providing me with an appropriate environment for my now complex disabilities, was suggested as an ideal solution. It was agreed that my own home was no longer suitable to accommodate the equipment I needed, as it was too small and compact. The annex would be built for my needs now and, in the years to come, as I got older. This included it being able to accommodate a hoist, which I really didn't want to even think about. The thought of having to use a hoist, even if in the future, was not something I wanted to comprehend. Yes, I'd had to use one at the start of my journey, but I'd hated it and could not contemplate having to ever use one again. It was also hard to think that the home that I'd just spent two years renovating, inside and out, for my planned future, was no longer suitable for the me now. But what did the future hold for me now, as I had no idea of what lay ahead. But I couldn't afford to dwell on this, so I chose not to.

*

My electric wheelchair arrived at the ward. I soon discovered that it was too small for me, but until it could be swapped for another one, I would keep it for now. What a difference it made to my ability to be more independent in getting around my room and going to the gym for physio. Kerry no longer had to come to get me and push me in my manual wheelchair. However, I still didn't feel brave enough to use it to go down on the elevator on my own, to the café or the shop, and as I couldn't open the doors. I couldn't have done that anyway. I also couldn't use it when going out in the car with family or friends, as it was too big and didn't fold up to be put in the boot.

On one occasion, Kim and Sean arranged for a special taxi that could accommodate my wheelchair, to pick me up from the hospital and take me to my neighbours' garden for a barbecue, as I could access their garden but not my own. Kim came to the hospital to accompany me in the taxi and I had a lovely time, feeling part of the outside world again. When the taxi came to take me back to the hospital, my neighbours were around to wave me off and I felt very emotional. It highlighted how my life was now. I wasn't the same as all these people around me, I was now severely disabled and my life had changed forever. But I remained strong, especially as Kim was in the taxi with me and she had arranged this special treat just for me. How could I let her see me upset? She would have felt she was to blame and she wasn't.

More fundraising events took place just before I was scheduled to go to Ninewells. There were even a couple of Radio interviews done with the event organisers and for one of the interviews, I was asked in advance to provide a couple of my favourite songs. It felt surreal, hearing them talk about me on the radio and to hear them play my chosen songs as I listened to them from my hospital bed. I found it hard to register that they were talking about me. The world I now found myself in, wasn't the world I was used to and I often thought that I would wake up back in the real world and be Marguerite Henderson again. I didn't feel like me anymore and I certainly didn't look like me, even if I'd had my limbs. I often told the staff this and showed them a photograph of me taken in December 2017, three months before I became unwell. I certainly didn't look like the same person.

Two big events took place on the same night, on the weekend before I was scheduled to go to Ninewells. A friend agreed to represent me at the 'Music for Marguerite' event at Pittencrieff Park in Dunfermline. The other one was being run by my local community at Lochore Institute and I decided to attend this one; I knew the venue and my friends had sent me a photo of the disabled toilet, so I knew that I could access this also. Acknowledging that I would have to plan all outings from now on, to make sure I could access places and use the facilities, was upsetting, as it reinforced that I could no longer be impulsive about visiting places I hadn't been to before.

On the date of the event, I began to panic at the prospect of attending and being seen in public. Only the organisers knew I was going, in case I changed my mind and also because I wanted to enter quietly, without any fuss.

My friends came to the hospital to get me and my stomach was churning. I arrived at the venue early and I was astonished at how beautifully decorated the hall was. I sat with my family and friends with my back to everyone else, as I knew if I faced them, I wouldn't have been able to cope. However, many people came over to speak to me and at times this was overwhelming, leaving me feeling a bit agitated. But I knew they just wanted to say hello and show support, which I so appreciated. I know they would have been shocked at how I looked and I realise that all the events taking place were due to how horrific what had happened to me was. But I couldn't think of that, as it would have been too upsetting to dwell on and of no benefit.

The show was amazing, but it was hard to watch people up dancing, as it emphasised that I now couldn't and maybe never would again. I remember sitting there feeling different from everyone else and trying hard not to get upset at the realisation that I would never socialise with people, as I had before. My disabilities would prevent this, no matter how much I wanted to. I couldn't walk between tables to talk to people, I couldn't access the bar and I couldn't even drink from a glass without a straw. I needed taken to the toilet and helped once there to use the Banana Board to get on and off. And the Banana Board wasn't something you could transport discretely.

During the evening, the event organisers requested a photograph be taken with myself and them. This was a big ask, as I'd never liked getting my photo taken in the first place, but now due to how I looked, the thought of this made me panic and feel very exposed. I was having to face a hall full of people. But I couldn't say no, as they were all very kind and had been amazing in their efforts to raise money for me. Having my photo taken was the least I could do. Due to being in hospital, I had to leave the event early but on arriving at the hospital, I again found myself locked out, having to go to Accident & Emergency to get them to open the door to let me in. Once back in my room and in bed on my own, the emotions and feelings I'd managed to control during the evening, engulfed me and I sobbed. 'Who had I become?' I felt on the outside of the world I was once a part of. Looking in, knowing that I'd never be part of it again. The next morning, after tossing and turning all night, my mood was low. The staff asked how the night before had gone and I tried to put aside how I was feeling and focussed on how amazing the night had been. It had been organised just for me and had been a massive success with everyone having a great time and enjoying the camaraderie that only local people can enjoy when they get together. Later that morning, I went on Facebook, only to see a picture of me, taken the night before at the event, showing me with my amputated limbs and looking so unwell. It was the first time I'd seen a front view picture of myself and I felt my heart miss a beat. Any time I had left the hospital in my wheelchair, I'd deliberately turned away from the glass windows that line the front of the building, as I didn't want to see my reflection. The reality of how I now looked, now stared me in the face.

As I tried to keep calm, I read the comments people had posted, but reading the comment 'God Bless', which I know was not stated to offend, was too much for me to cope with and my tears flowed. A staff member tried to comfort me, telling me that people who saw me all the time, didn't see me as anyone other than Marguerite. I was still the same person I'd always been. But how could I be? I no longer looked like me, but like a freak of nature. I felt people now

Figure 18; Me at the Fundraising Event

looked at me with pity. I couldn't contemplate living as I was. It was too much to even think about and the thought of it scared me more than words can say.

*

That weekend I struggled with the ability to remain positive. I also struggled with my impending readmission to Ninewells Hospital on the Monday. I knew that when in Ninewells, I would not have the same number of visitors and worried about my ability to eat the meals. I'd hated it when I was there previously. The contents of my room were packed away - my cards and gifts, my television and my Alexa. My suitcase was packed, ready for my departure. The starkness of the room that had been my home for some time now was upsetting, as it highlighted that I would be leaving my safe haven in the morning and facing yet another challenge.

*

On Monday the 18th of June, an ambulance took me back to Ninewells. My electric wheelchair was left behind, as the ambulance taking me to Ninewells couldn't accommodate it. I was admitted into a four-bay room, and as I'd always had my own room in Ward 33, this heightened my anxiety levels right away. I was already struggling to keep control. Kim met me in the ward and we waited for me to be admitted by a member of staff. I became upset as the nurse filled in my admission paperwork. Being back in Ninewells was really scary and I felt so vulnerable. I'd felt secure and safe in Ward 33, with staff that had been supporting me throughout my journey and knew me so well. They knew what tasks I could do myself and those I needed help with. Nobody knew me here and I felt so alone. The nurse recognised I was struggling to be in a bay of four beds and assured me that I'd be given my own room, when one became available.

The physio who had visited me when I'd been in Ninewells previously, when I'd had my legs amputated, came to see me. She made me aware that it would be her I'd be working with whilst there and that I'd be going to the gym twice daily, during my stay.

One thing that I shouldn't have worried about was not getting plenty of visitors. I was out most lunch times and then again at tea time, for the duration of my stay. In fact, the staff got me to sign a form acknowledging that I took full responsibility for my own safety when not on the ward because I was out so often.

I was fitted with my prosthetic legs on the afternoon of my first day in Ninewells and I can't describe the feelings that I felt, standing up in them for the first time. I must admit that to begin with, I was deflated and upset, when I realised how intricate my prosthetic legs were. I don't know what I thought they would be like, but I definitely didn't think they would have so many parts. First, there was the Iceross, which was a silicon sock that had a rivet on the end of it. Next was a woolly sock, then a foam mould of my leg, then another woolly sock. Finally, the prosthetic leg was put on, clicking into place by the rivet being embedded in a hole, in the inside of the prosthetic leg. If my stumps shrunk during the day, as they often did, another sock needed to be added to keep the leg fitting snuggly. I remember trying hard to keep the tears from flowing, as I tried to come to terms with how complicated the legs were to put on and knowing I would never be able to put the legs on myself, having only one hand and no fingers. Even taking them off was too hard for me at that time. It reinforced that no matter what progress I made in the months that followed, I would always need help putting them on and recognising this, was heart-wrenching. But I knew I had to be strong and look at the positives and not dwell on what I couldn't change. I could stand, I could walk, with the aid of the gutter frame, so for the first time since I lost my legs, I could think about being in control of my own mobility, instead of being pushed in a wheelchair.

Standing up needed strength, as I needed to pull myself up, using the muscles in the top of my legs, as well as my upper arms. I had acquired this strength because of the fantastic work Kerry had done with me, during my physio sessions, working on my core muscles and balance in particular. Putting this to use, to balance on my prosthetic legs, took a lot of strength and energy. But most of all, it took confidence in my ability to stand up straight and walk, putting one foot in front of the other, while walking on legs that were not natural parts of my body. The use of a gutter frame to help keep me balanced, was essential at this

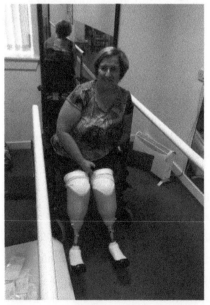

Figure 19;
Wearing Prosthetic Legs for the first time.

stage. Oh, how thankful I was, that my amputations had been done below the knee on both legs. I now understood how difficult it would have been for me to achieve walking, without my knees to help me balance.

I remained in the four bedded bay that night, but was moved to a single room the next morning. Although the room was uninviting, it did mean I had my own space, which reduced my anxiety of feeling that people were looking at me. I hated people seeing me wriggling on and off

Figure 20;
Standing in my new legs, using a Gutter Frame

and up and down the bed, so being in my own room prevented this and made me feel less vulnerable in an environment that was alien and totally out of my comfort zone.

However, the toilet in the room was too small and inaccessible for me, so if I needed to go to the toilet, I had to be wheeled down to the communal toilet on a commode, which felt humiliating. The commode was a lot lighter than the freeway chair I used in Ward 33 and made me feel unsafe. I also had to use the commode chair when having a shower, which also wasn't in my room, so I'd again be wheeled along the corridor to the communal shower, wrapped in my dressing gown to hide my amputated limbs.

The staff in the ward at Ninewells didn't know me and I had to ask for help all the time. I didn't have to do that in Ward 33, as they knew what tasks I could and couldn't do. Having to state what I couldn't do for myself all the time, reinforced to me how much support I needed and this was bad for my self-esteem. Continuing to remain positive took a lot of effort.

If it wasn't for my family and friends visiting me every day and taking me out for lunch or dinner, I don't think I'd have coped.

Whilst in Ninewells, I attended physio twice daily, in the morning and in the afternoon. Walking on two prosthetic legs was very scary and the thought of falling was constantly at the back of my mind. But I so wanted to walk and gave a hundred percent commitment at every physio session. My physio once told me that I never said no to whatever she asked me to try to do, but I knew that if I said no and thought about each of her requests and how risky they were, I would probably never have done it. The result would then have meant that I would not have progressed as quickly as I did. It also meant that I'd have to remain in Ninewells for longer and I didn't want that!

My confidence in walking improved, but I soon recognised that having only a partial right hand meant using gutter crutches was unachievable. I couldn't hold the left crutch, so using it was unsafe. It was therefore agreed, that I would need to use a gutter frame. Part of my time at physio was to learn to stand and do an activity at a work bench, as this would help me progress in the future to achieve tasks at home. One day, when my friends Mary and Raymond visited, we spent time in the hospital garden, planting bedding plants and threading sweet peas through a trellis. This was to have me use my hand and progress using my small motor skills. I was also given putty to squeeze to build up the strength in my hand, as my hand was very weak. I had minimal ability to hold or lift anything of any weight.

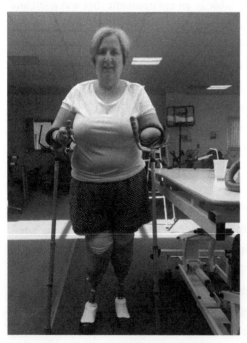

Figure 21; Using Gutter Crutches at Ninewells

During my time at Ninewells, my friends came to collect me to attend The Benarty Gala, a big event in my local community's calendar. A raffle was to be drawn in my name, as part of my fundraising campaign, and Kim, Emma, family and friends manned a stall to raise additional funds. It was a beautiful sunny day and although I was really nervous about being in the public eye at such a big event, with my missing limbs being in full view for everyone to see, I was still determined to attend, to show my appreciation for the support from my amazing community. My friends came to collect me from Ninewells and on arriving home, my electric wheelchair was waiting for me. Sean had gone down to Ward 33 to collect it in his work van. I remember watching the parade, feeling apprehensive, as I saw the crowds of people in attendance, when a friend and her two sisters stopped to speak to me. She quickly made me feel more relaxed when she made me laugh, by saying she was sick of seeing my face in the paper. My reply was to state that I was too. I had been in the press quite a lot, not only because of what had happened to me, but also because of the number of fundraising events that had been taking place. Anyway, I had a lovely time at the Gala, spending most of the time talking to friends and neighbours, who wanted to wish me well. I was tired when I arrived back at Ninewells, as I was still recovering and got tired easily. It had been a long day and it had taken its toll on me. However, I went to bed contented, with a sense of achievement, having faced the outside world in such a massive way.

On the 28th of June, I had progressed so well with my walking, that the decision was made for me to return to Kirkcaldy and Ward 33. I had been in Ninewells for only 10 days, a much shorter period than had been anticipated.

I arrived back from Ninewells to an amazing reception from the Ward 33 staff. They had made sure that I got my old room back and had 'Welcome Back' posters on the wall and toilet door. It felt like I'd arrived home, where I belonged. I soon had it looking homely again, with my personal bits and bobs back in place and my television and Alexa tuned in and up and running.

For the first time since I had arrived on the ward on the 19th of March, I could stand. The staff had only seen me sitting in a bed or in my wheelchair, so seeing me stand was an emotional moment for both them and for me. There were a few tears and lots of cuddles.

But my first week end back in Ward 33 was not a good one. Ongoing issues with a close family member came to a head on the Saturday evening. I was left so distraught that the nursing staff had to give me an injection to relieve the nausea I was experiencing because of the stress and anxiety. I could not stop crying and staff stayed with me until I settled then checked on me during the night. By the Sunday morning, I had hit rock bottom and felt I no longer wanted to be alive. I felt I was to blame for all the issues that were affecting my family. I knew they were all struggling with what had happened to me and I could sense the tension between some of them. I couldn't help feeling that if I had died, none of the animosity would have occurred. I recognised that some of the relationships within my family were going to sever and I couldn't understand how this could happen, or how they could let this happen. I felt their issues were paltry in comparison to what I was going through and I wondered why they couldn't recognise that and think that I would want to listen to silly issues which could so easily be fixed. Couldn't they see I had enough to cope with, trying to deal with the horrific outcomes of contracting sepsis? My problems would never be fixed as my legs and arms would never grow back.

Sunday morning came and I remained in bed, refusing to shower, or have breakfast, lunch or tea. I just lay in bed and sobbed and the tears wouldn't stop. Nursing staff sat with me and I knew they were worried. I had always focussed on remaining strong, but I didn't have the strength to fight how low I was feeling. My friend phoned and recognised by my voice that I wasn't in a good place, so she and another friend came to see me. She told me months afterwards, that she had been very upset on seeing how sad and distraught I was that Sunday evening. She had felt angry that one of my family could cause me to look so vulnerable and broken. I remember Emma coming in with food and encouraging me to eat something, butt every mouthful was hard to swallow.

By the Monday morning, when my consultant and her team visited me on the doctor's round, I wasn't in the mood to talk and lay facing the wall. Kerry and Tracey came back to see me on my own later and agreed I needed help. However, enquiries into me accessing psychological help proved futile, as this, we found out, could only be achieved once I was out of hospital. My life felt hopeless. Up to this point, I had used lots of psychological strategies to help me cope. I had learned these through my job as a Family Support Worker, but I knew I was out of my depth now and needed professional help. Being aware that the help I needed wasn't available, made me frightened and helpless. I had no idea how I was going to move forward and regain the ability to continue to fight what this illness had done to me. Months later, when discussing this episode with Kerry, she told me, that when she saw me lying in my bed, facing the wall, she knew I had hit rock bottom. She said she knew the day would come, when being strong and positive, would be too hard for me to keep up, but seeing me, lying there facing the wall, was still hard for her to witness.

It was then that Tracey arranged for me to meet Lynne. Lynne is the charge nurse for the mental health liaison service. She normally works with outpatients, but was brought in because of my exceptional circumstances. At our first meeting, Lynne could tell that I was very aware of how the psychological effects of what had happened to me, were impacting on my mental health. Our sessions thereafter were of great help to me. It gave me the chance to speak openly about how I was feeling, and work through my emotions and feelings with her. I soon became reliant on Lynne's support. However, it did take me some time before I divulged what had triggered my anxiety and emotional breakdown. I still continue to meet with Lynne and her support has been invaluable. She has been with me throughout most of my journey. I can talk to her openly about how hard it is to live without arms and legs and also about the ongoing issues within my family. They affect me so much on a daily basis and at times cause me so much more stress and anxiety than my severe disabilities do. I think that's because I can accept that contracting sepsis could not be helped, it was an illness. But other barriers and issues I've had to deal with along the way, could have been so easily avoided and therefore I find these harder to accept or come to terms with.

CHAPTER 13

July, My Rehabilitation Begins

Although my hand had more or less healed, a small scab, where my pinkie had been, became infected, possibly as a result of my time gardening whilst at Ninewells. This meant I was prescribed a course of antibiotics to make sure the dreaded sepsis did not return. I began to recognise any infection I contracted would set off alarm bells and this is still the case, with me being prescribed antibiotics if risk of infection is of concern. As I so much just want to be the same as everyone else, I wish this wasn't the case, but acknowledging that what happened to me was sepsis at its extreme, it's no wonder that making sure I don't contract it again is a priority. I know any health issues will be monitored closely.

I was still being prescribed Fragmin injections daily, to prevent blood clots, due to my limited mobility. I had the daily injections into my stomach and I hated them, as they would sting. I was also still getting blood taken every two days, most of the time. Making sure my organs were working properly and my blood was free from infection was still a priority and I understood that. Giving blood samples became routine to me and I developed friendships with the two phlebotomists. Even now if I see them in the hospital, when I'm there for my physio sessions, they always stop to chat and ask me how I'm doing.

I attended physio with Kerry every morning and knew the strength in my legs had improved. I steadily gained confidence daily in my ability to walk. I now walked in my room using my gutter frame and it was so much easier to go to the toilet, even if I still needed help to remove my trousers and pants. However, during the month of July, I was determined to achieve wiping my bottom on my own. I could do this when I went for a wee, but having no fingers meant that I still needed help to wipe my back passage and I hated it. It was so degrading and highlighted how much I needed help. However, I was determined to do this chore on my own and with lots of practice, I eventually conquered this task. I remember a colleague visiting me and asking what new skill I'd achieved that week and me informing her that I now could wipe my own derriere. I think she was shocked at my revelation, but it was massive for me, as I felt I was doing a yoga session to achieve this. The effort it took to do this task, and continues to be, can be exhausting, but to be independent, it's a necessity.

As mentioned earlier in my story, my left arm had become stiff and I was virtually unable to move it. Kerry had put tape on it to see if that helped, but it didn't work. So, I continued to do the exercises Kerry had given me to hopefully give it some flexibility, as it was affecting my ability to get my clothes on.

As I recovered, I was continually reminded of how much my daily routines had changed and this had a massive effect on my self-esteem. I no longer recognised myself and didn't know who I was anymore. Tracey understood this and we had a long chat, with me talking her through, who I had been before sepsis. I had loved my clothes and planned what I wore daily. I made sure I had matching jewellery, coordinated footwear and handbag and lastly, that my nails and make up were done. I recognised that there were some aspects of my life that were no longer achievable. Clothes were now bought for function, my shoes needed to be able to be worn with my prosthetic legs, changing handbags was too hard for me to achieve and as for changing my jewellery, without fingers, I just couldn't. Of course, having no fingers meant I had no finger nails, so I couldn't have my nails painted. That was devastating for me, as I'd always had my nails done on a monthly basis. Even wearing long necklaces wasn't possible, as they just got in my way and hindered my ability to do everyday tasks.

I could however still wear make-up and Tracey suggested that my makeup was brought in and applied every morning, after my shower.

I was determined to apply my own make-up, and although my hand was still very sensitive and had minimal strength, within a short period of time I'd mastered this task, much to the staff's astonishment, even managing to apply my own eyeliner and mascara.

I still needed help to dry and straighten my hair, as the hairdryer and straighteners were too heavy for me to hold for any length of time. I attempted to do both these tasks also, as I recognised that it was only by persevering that I would eventually achieve success.

*

I had come so far and had achieved much more than I, or any of the staff, had envisaged, but I knew that that there were many tasks I would never be able to achieve, no matter how hard I tried. I would need help from others for the rest of my life. This was hard to acknowledge, and even harder to continue to always see the positives and refrain from focussing on the negatives. That's when the staff on the ward helped me so much, as they would help me see the funny side of situations which occurred as a result of my lack of limbs. I remember one occasion during my frequent chats with the male nurse, which always resulted in us joking about my situation. I said to him, "Tell me something positive about having no limbs." He left my room unable to give me a reply, but sometime later popped his head around the door to say he had thought of something, stating that 'I'd make a good Halloween decoration'. Only he could have the courage to say that to me, but he knew I would see the funny side of the joke. We had the same warped sense of humour. I did tell him I'd get him back for his joke and I did.

The weather was glorious for most of the time during the months of April, May and June and the lovely weather conditions continued into July. Family and friends continued to take me out of the hospital on most days. We went for drives around Fife, going to places I'd never been to for years. I remember on one occasion, taking my two granddaughters to a play area with my auntie and uncle and how hard that was, not being able to push the girls on the swings, or help them on the other play equipment. The realisation of probably never being able to do these simple, but precious tasks was difficult to come to terms with, and I found it hard not to cry. Whilst at the park, a little girl came over to me and asked me where my arms and legs were. Her mum was mortified and apologised for her daughter, which was not necessary. She was an inquisitive child, who only wanted to know why my limbs were missing and I told her, that I had been unwell and they had been removed to make me well again. It was the first time I had been asked this question and it wouldn't be the last. To be honest, I find being asked out right, easier than people continually staring at me. Even over a year later, I still find people looking at me hard to accept and upsetting and I think I always will. But I need to ignore it as best I can, if I want to make the most of my life and leave the security of the indoors and face the outside world.

I also remember passing a beach with Erin and Gracie one day, when out in the car and Erin getting all excited at the prospect of playing in the sand. As I was there, we couldn't let her do this, as I couldn't access the beach. Again, it highlighted how I'd never be able to play with the girls on the beach and there were other things I'd never be able to do too, like walk in the sand, feeling it between my toes, or walk in the sea, feeling it splash around my ankles. Every day would highlight things I would never be able to achieve again and this made keeping positive difficult. But I knew I needed to keep focussing on the things I could achieve or hoped to achieve, to enable me to remain strong and continue to be positive and achieve being as independent as possible.

When going out for something to eat, I became more aware of the foods I could eat independently and stayed away most of the time from any foods that needed to be cut, as I was not able to use a knife. Spaghetti and tagliatelle were out of the question, as I couldn't wrap the pasta around my fork. Burgers and some sandwiches were also off limits, as I didn't have the span on my right hand to hold them. I tended to choose fish on most occasions, as I could cut it with my fork.

Drinks were also problematic. Coffee cups with small handles were unmanageable for me, as I only had half a thumb to hold it with, so I would ask for a mug or a latte glass. I couldn't lift a glass, so I used a straw, if drinking juice. However, I have no problem holding a wine glass, which was a bonus, so a glass of wine was often consumed.

The construction of my new home began in July. Added on to the side of Sean and Kim's house, it would be built to accommodate my needs and enable me to be as independent as possible. I must admit, I had mixed emotions about it, as it was another life-changing event. I knew my new home was where I needed to be, but it felt scary and surreal. But for now, my home was in Ward 33, where I felt secure and protected.

Each morning, the staff put on my Alexa and got me ready for the day ahead along to music. When I first came back from Ninewells, Kerry would come to put my legs on, but the staff took over this task. Putting my legs on could prove difficult and although it caused much hilarity, at times I'm sure, they could have thrown them out of the window.

I went out for my meals most days, but if in the ward at meal times, I could select from my store of food in the ward fridge. However, if I had to eat the hospital food, I had been made aware from the catering staff that I could ask for foods which were not on the menu. So, for lunch I'd ask for a toastie or a panini and for tea, a baked potato. Sometimes at the weekends, the staff would include me if they were having bacon or sausage on a roll at breakfast time, or if they were ordering a McDonalds during the night. I remember one day, Dominoes were parked at the hospital for the day, with the staff each getting a free pizza. I wasn't staff, but they made sure I had one too, with me and Emma enjoying it for our tea.

The decision had been made that I would be medically retired from my work. It would take a few weeks for this to be processed and I knew it was the right decision, as I knew I was no longer able to do my job. However, it made me so sad, as I'd loved my job and had planned to continue working for a few years yet. I had recognised that during my time in hospital, visits from my work colleagues had fallen away, with only a few now visiting regularly. This made me feel that I was no longer seen as part of the staff, but as a former staff member. However, I was grateful to the people who did visit and tried not to dwell on why others didn't.

Not being able to return to work, meant I would be entitled to Disability Benefits and this was applied for. Filling in the forms was difficult, as I had to record how disabled I was. I had been told that I only needed twelve points to receive Disability Allowance and being assessed as having forty-seven points was mind-blowing. It was of no surprise that I was awarded Disability Allowance, but unfortunately, I would not receive any payments until I left hospital.

CHAPTER 14

August and Getting Ready for Home

At the beginning of August, I was to attend a family wedding. My family had helped me get an outfit to wear, bringing it into the hospital for me to try on, as trying on clothes in a shop was totally out of the question. Not being able to go shopping for my own wedding outfit upset me, but I just had to accept this. I did go shopping for sandals and accessories and I was aware of people looking at the surreal situation they were witnessing. Me sitting in a wheelchair, trying on sandals, wearing prosthetic legs, that consisted of steel poles and plastic feet.

Just before the day of the wedding, I was standing at the sink, washing my hands. I'd always been in my wheelchair whilst at the sink previously, so all I had seen in the mirror, above the sink up until then, had been my head. Now, however, I noticed the underside of my left amputated arm, looked flabby and shapeless. Although I recognised that this was due to the muscles having been cut in half, when my arm was operated on, how it looked still took me aback. My friend the male nurse came into my room at that point and asked what was up and I showed him my stump, stating,

Figure 22;
My Silver Sandals and Painted Toenails.

that I'd have to keep my arm flat on the arm rest of my wheelchair, when I went to the wedding, as I didn't want anyone to see it, as my stump looked like a hot dog roll, without the hot dog. I should have known his reaction would not be empathetic, as our friendship was built on having a similar sense of humour and being honest, so his response was to say, "Marguerite, I think, they'll be more concerned that you haven't got a hand at the bottom of your stump." He certainly knew how to bring me back to reality, but it was what I needed. He never let my disabilities, get in the way of seeing me, Marguerite the person and it made me feel normal. I found it hard to be constantly treated with pity, with people treading on eggs shells, frightened to say the wrong thing. Anyway, his answer to the problem, was for me to get two eyes and a tongue tattooed on the end of my stump and then people would have something to look at. His suggestion and the image of my stump being tattooed in this way, still makes me laugh and I often wish I had the courage to have it done. It would show the world that I still have a sense of humour, even after having my limbs amputated and possibly break down the barriers when people see me for the first time and don't know how to react and talk to me.

The day of the wedding arrived and I woke up feeling anxious about going, as I knew I was attending an event with lots of people I didn't know. It was yet another first, going out of my comfort zone. I knew people would look at me: it was hard not to look at me, looking the way I did and I'd probably have done the same, if the roles were reversed. But it was still upsetting for me and continues to be upsetting, up to the present day.

After showering, the staff helped me to get dressed, with Alexa playing in the background while I sipped a glass of wine. This was what I would normally have done if I'd been at home when preparing to go to a wedding, and the staff wanted me to feel as normal as possible. A staff member did my hair and helped me with my makeup and jewellery. Then Emma arrived with our lunch, which we ate in my room, before heading off to the wedding. I was petrified.

I was keen to be as inconspicuous as possible, so decided to go to the toilet on arrival. Going to the toilet when out of the ward was a big issue for me and I would limit my fluid intake to avoid having to find a disabled toilet. Today was no different, even though I had known in advance that a disabled toilet was available. Anyway, I asked a member of staff where the toilet was, only to discover it could only be accessed through where the ceremony was to take place. This meant that some of the decorated chairs, which had been set out for the ceremony, had to be moved. Before I could say, "Don't bother," chairs were scraping along the floor, being moved to create a pathway to the toilet. The noise seemed to echo loudly and people were looking to see what was happening. I was mortified. After going to the toilet and retracing my route through the chairs, I recognised there would not be room for me to be at the ceremony in my wheelchair. The staff were willing to try and fit my chair in, but I made the decision to stay in the lounge area, where I could still see the bride arriving and listen to the ceremony.

I refrained from getting my photo taken, not wanting to see a picture of myself. I still had that vision in my head of the photo of me, taken at the charity event in June. I didn't want to feel as I had done then, ever again.

Even though I felt different and looked different from all the other guests in attendance, having been to many restaurants as an amputee I coped well with the meal, but the tea and coffee was served in a separate reception room, with no tables, so to be able to drink my coffee, I needed to find a spot where I could put the cup down on my right-hand side. I didn't have the strength or the ability to hold a cup for any length of time.

When the music began, I knew I needed to leave. Sitting in a wheelchair, watching my family and the other guests dancing, was too much for me to deal with. Emma drove me back to the hospital, my family waving me off and looking so perplexed. I knew they recognised how much life had changed for me and for them. My exit emphasised the togetherness we had lost and could never get back.

On the journey back to the hospital, I found it hard to keep it together, as I didn't want Emma to see me upset. My auntie and uncle were in my room when I arrived back in the ward. They knew how hard the day had been for me and wanted to make sure I was alright. The staff made us all a cuppa and they stayed for a while to keep me company. As soon as they left, I could not keep my tears back any longer. What had I become and what was to become of me? I was scared of what the future held for me, but what I did know, was that it wasn't the future that I wanted. I wanted the life I had before sepsis had struck. I didn't want to live as a quadruple amputee, no longer able to do the things that everyone takes for granted.

I cried myself to sleep that night and when I awoke on the Sunday morning, my mood was low and I remained in bed, just needing to be on my own. The wedding had highlighted yet again, that I was no longer the same as everyone else and never would be. I felt bereaved. I felt I had lost another aspect of living that I'd taken for granted.

A nurse suggested I have a bubbly bath. I'd had a bath on the ward on a couple of occasions, since my wounds had healed. The first time, Kerry had panicked at how hot I'd had the water, but I'd enjoyed relaxing in it, with my music on and a magazine to read. It was a big bath that moved up and down, with a special chair, making it reasonably easy for me to get into. Anyway, I agreed to having a bath, with lots of bubbles, and with my favourite music playing in the background. I took a magazine with me, so that I could read while relaxing in the hot soapy water. But the bath did not help my mood and I lay there, crying silent tears of despair. I put my head under the water and thought that if I stayed there my life would soon be over. I felt that my life wasn't worth living anymore and that I no longer wanted to live. I felt my lungs expanding and my need to breathe became more and more desperate. I couldn't go through with it. A nurse came into the bathroom and said she had realised I had been in the bath for a long time and had come to check that I was alright. She made a joke about being frightened I had drowned; little did she know how close I'd been to making that a reality. I've often thought about that day and it frightens me to think how much I'd wanted to die, ending the nightmare that my life had become. Although I still have my low times, I've never felt suicidal again. When times are tough, I do think that, if I'd never come out of that coma, I would have been unaware of dying and that would have been so much easier than the daily struggles I now had to endure. But I know that my family needs me, and their needs will always come before my own.

My bath time experience gave me the jolt I needed to focus on trying as much as I could, to not dwell on the things I couldn't achieve but focus on building on the skills I could possibly achieve, whatever they were.

Another event in August, that challenged me accessing the outside world, was a trip to the cinema to watch, ' Mama Mia, Here We Go Again', with Kim and my granddaughter Erin. I was in my manual wheelchair, as we waited in the queue to buy our tickets. I was surrounded by everyone standing around me and felt probably how children in buggies must feel, looking at everyone's body, instead of their faces, as they towered above. When it was our turn to go to the desk, Kim, pushed me towards it, then turned me around in my chair, so I had my back to her, but facing everyone in the queue. I recognised, that I would do this, when I used to push my mum in her wheelchair, probably so that I didn't have to manoeuvre the chair after being served but could just walk away. Now with being the person in the chair, I understood how vulnerable it made you feel. There I was, facing everyone, in a wheelchair, with steel poles for legs, a missing arm and a deformed hand, with everyone staring at me. Kim quickly turned me around when I asked her to, so that I had my back to them. I know she hadn't meant to make me feel uncomfortable. I had made the same mistake when I took my mum out in her wheelchair. It was a lack of understanding the plight of people who are wheelchair bound.

As we sat in the disabled seats at the front of the cinema, Erin asked me if I wanted some of her popcorn. I put my hand in the box, but none came out. I couldn't grasp any. Erin had to put a piece at a time on the palm of my hand, to allow me to eat some. I could have become upset, failing at yet another task, but I focussed on the main purpose of being there - to be at the cinema with my daughter and granddaughter.

I continued to do the exercises Kerry had given me to improve the mobility in my left arm, but it hadn't worked. Kerry asked a colleague who specialised in orthopaedics to examine my arm and he diagnosed it as a possible frozen shoulder. Kerry and I had also thought this. It was probably as a result of me not using my arm enough. The consultant confirmed it was a frozen shoulder and gave me three options for treating the condition. One, I could continue to have physio from Kerry. Two, I could have a cortisone injection. Or three, I could have an operation to manipulate my arm, with the hope it would stretch the tendons and muscles. The risk with this procedure, however, was that my arm might be broken, and I'd arrive back from surgery with a plaster cast on. I decided to go ahead with option three and therefore, the operation was scheduled for a couple of days later. The day of operation number four arrived and I was taken to theatre. I remember a nurse asking me if I remembered I was being operated on that day, as I was so calm. I think after what I'd been through, another operation didn't faze me. It couldn't be any worse than what I'd already been through. I woke up after the operation feeling a little tired, but with no other after-affects from the anaesthetics. A big bonus was that my arm hadn't been broken and was not in a plaster cast. The operation was an instant success, with my arm so much more mobile. During the next few weeks my ability to use it improved, with me doing the exercises given to me by the orthopaedic physio to increase its flexibility. The pain I'd felt in my arm also disappeared completely over time.

Another complication of being in hospital for so long and getting my temperature taken every day and having the thermometer placed in my ear, was that my ears became blocked. I think the thermometer had been pushing the wax into my ears, so my hearing was impaired and I felt light-headed. Ear drops were prescribed twice daily and given in the morning and in the evening, alleviating the problem within a few days.

My walking improved too and I practised walking up and down the corridor in the ward, using my gutter frame. After each physio session in the gym, Kerry walked me back towards my room, with me using no aids to help me walk. Every day, I walked a bit further and by the time I was discharged from the hospital, I could walk all the way back to my room, which was approximately sixty metres in length. As I walked with Kerry, we sang songs that had walking in the lyrics. Songs such as, 'Walking Back to Happiness', 'I'm Walking on Sunshine' and 'I'm Gonna Be (500 Miles)' to name but a few. Doing this stopped me from focussing on the possibility of falling and instead focus on the words of the songs. It worked.

Kerry also began to have me practise going up steps, with a set of four steps being available for me to practise on in the gym. Lifting my prosthetic legs up onto each step was difficult. They were so heavy, although, I have been informed by my prosthetist that they weigh twenty percent less than what my own legs would have weighed. But with practice I was able to master this, although I still found going downstairs more difficult, as I feel less in control of my balance. I remember one day, standing with Kerry at the top of the practice stairs, which had a handrail around the top step. Both of us standing there reminded me of the scene from the movie, The Titanic, where Rose and Jack were standing at the front of the ship, their arms spread out as if they were flying. I started to sing the theme song, acting out the scene and Kerry joined in too. I'm sure, anyone entering the gym at that moment, would have wondered what was going on. To be honest, taking the seriousness out of situations, helped me cope and gave me the positive attitude to achieve success, no matter what that was.

During my time in hospital, Kerry had been the one to keep me positive, focussed and on track. She was my rock and knew me so well and so I felt I could be honest with her about how I was really feeling at times. I know I put a brave face on to my family, friends and the staff in the ward, even when I felt low, but I didn't with her. Maybe it's because I knew she'd see right through me, as I think she knew me better than I knew myself. She was also very honest and would tell me it, as it was. I remember one day, me moaning about how hard life was and her telling me that if I hadn't had my limbs amputated, I would have died. That I now had to focus on living, I had survived and my kids needed me. She was right and now, any time when I feel down, I remember her timely words.

During one of our chats, I mentioned that I still had little recollection of my time in ICU. Kerry suggested we visit there and arranged it for a time that the staff who had cared for me would be on duty. I was nervous as I went down in the lift, and as we walked along the corridor that would take me to ICU, Kerry explained that when I was a patient in the unit, the snow had been half way up the outside of the glass, in the corridor. Due to The Beast from the East having arrived in Scotland.

She showed me pictures on her phone of the snow, making me aware of how it would have looked to my family, when they visited me.

The staff who nursed me were there to greet me, but I couldn't remember them. Nor could I remember the bed I had occupied during my time there. The visit did not trigger any memories, but I appreciated being able to see where my journey had begun.

The day came when the decision was made that it was time for me to prepare for going home. I was now in good health and my rehabilitation was going well. A Care Plan would have to be completed to assess my new set of needs and a meeting was arranged to discuss this. I had completed Children's Plans as part of my job, so knew it would be a similar document, looking at a holistic approach to make sure all my needs were met.

Myself, Kim, Sean, Kerry, Tracey, Lynne and the Community Occupational Therapist attended the meeting and it was agreed that my discharge from hospital would take place within the next two to three weeks. However, a package of care was still to be identified, as there were concerns about how I would manage go to the toilet by myself, as I still hadn't managed the task of pulling up my own pants and trousers. One suggestion was for me to wear a skirt and no pants. I'd never been a skirt person, but to wear one with no pants was not an option for me, nor my family. I knew I couldn't be in company feeling undressed and undignified. I knew that to avoid this, or to prevent ongoing issues with me getting to the toilet during the day, when my family were at work, I had to achieve pulling up my own pants and trousers. First off, my sister-in-law, sewed hoops from ribbon on to both sides of my pants, to see if that worked, but it didn't. Eventually, I discovered that, if I wore bigger sized pants and trousers, to allow me to get my hand and stump inside them, then I would be able to pull them up. Once I practised this task, I soon became adept at it. I no longer needed help from staff. This meant the concerns around me going to the toilet once I went home, were no longer an issue. It was agreed that, due to the support I had from my family and friends, I would get care from ICASS (Integrated Community Assessment & Support Services) until an Initial Assessment was completed by Social Work, to assess my long-term needs,

Every morning Kerry came to the door of my room and said, "Nice bed head Marguerite!" She'd bring me a real coffee and pour it into my personal coffee mug. Once I'd drank it, I'd wash and dry my cup and put it back on the shelf, where I kept my own jar of coffee, as I didn't like the coffee the hospital provided. I'd fathomed out a way to open the waste paper bin in my room, by using an extendable back scratcher I'd been given as a present. I used the back scratcher to prize the lid open and then hold it between my knees, to hold the lid ajar, until I 'd put my rubbish in it, with my right hand. I've never figured out, why I was provided with a pedal bin in my room, when I had no feet to press the pedal.

I also started laying out my clothes for the morning before I went to bed for the night. It took a lot of effort to do that, as balancing whilst bending over was difficult and holding coat hangers using my right hand was hard, as it was still weak and sensitive. But I was determined to do as much as possible for myself.

I couldn't dress myself, but I was able to undress and put my night-dress on at bed time. I could not do this if I had a bra on, so I started to wear sports bras, which went over my head, as they were easier to remove. However, I could not get my legs off on my own and the staff would do that chore for me.

*

Another achievement was to thread a needle and darn a small hole in my cardigan. I used a big needle, and stuck it into a plastic cup to keep it steady, while I threaded it. I managed to then tie a knot in the end of the thread, after a few attempts, before using my stump to hold my cardigan while I darned it. A staff member asked what I was doing. When she realised, I was sewing, she couldn't believe it and gave me a cuddle. It wasn't long before the jungle drums went around the ward and other staff came into my room to congratulate me.

This was a massive achievement for me. As I had explained in the introduction of my story, my hobby had been sewing and the thought of not being able to sew again was a huge blow. I found it hard to accept, so even managing to darn a small hole in my cardigan was something to be proud of.

After your legs are amputated, the swelling can continue to reduce, and I had been made aware that this could take an average of up to two years. This meant my prosthetic legs would need changed frequently. I knew my legs were shrinking, as I needed more socks on with them to make them fit better. I remember on a few occasions walking along the corridor on the ward, with the aid of my gutter frame and my legs moving, making my feet point outwards. This would cause hilarity, as I ended up walking like Charlie Chaplin, with jokes about me not needing to turn my gutter frame to go into my room, as my feet were facing that way anyway. On one occasion, when my feet went squint, a nurse walking behind me laughed, stating she could see the nail varnish on my prosthetic toes, as my feet were facing sideways.

The type of Iceross I had been given caused friction blisters to appear on my legs and I needed two or three dressings on each leg, to protect the blisters and enable me to continue to wear them.

So Kerry contacted Ninewells and an appointment was arranged for me to have my legs recast. I would receive my new legs once they were made. I was given a different type of Iceross too, which was more pliable and not so damaging to my legs. At the appointment, I was also given an Iceross for my left arm and was cast for a prosthetic arm too, which I would receive in due course. However, I was given the Iceross with me and asked to wear it for a short time each day, to get my arm used to wearing it and also to make sure there was no irritation to my skin. Although my skin had no negative reaction to the Iceross, it was hot to wear. It was made of plastic and the hot weather that summer made it feel uncomfortable. I remember one day, my friend visiting me whilst I was wearing it and it being time to take it off. As I slid it off my stump, a pool of water poured out of it and landed on my bedside table, as my arm had been sweating so much.

As I had been awarded PIP (Personal Independence Payment), which I would be entitled to receive once I was discharged from hospital, I could now apply for a Blue Disability Badge. The badge would be of so much benefit, allowing me to park in disabled spaces. It would allow my family and friends to park outside the main entrance to the hospital when they came to pick me up and take me out for the day, or to park in disabled spaces, where ever we were going.

It also meant I could look at getting a mobility car that could accommodate my electric wheelchair. The nearest dealer that provided a car for my needs was in Glasgow, so Sean, Kim and I took a trip through to have a look at what was available. We discovered that, due to me requiring a car with a ramp, to accommodate my electric wheelchair, I would have to pay a £3500 deposit towards it. I also was informed that, if, in the future, I ever wanted to drive a car that was adapted for me being in my electric wheelchair, it would be a £15,000 deposit. That made it impossible for me to ever consider driving by myself again. However, I now knew what cars were available to me and once I was discharged from hospital, I returned to order one.

During the month of August, I was informed by Fife Council of my retirement date. I would officially retire on medical grounds on the 7th of September. It was hard for me to take in and wasn't a decision I had been in control of. I planned to retire one day and enjoy holidays, weekend breaks, being a lady who lunched, but mostly, to have more time to spend with my family, relaxing and enjoying life. The prospect of retiring now, was not part of that plan and all the things I planned to do, would no longer be achievable. I was no longer able bodied, independent and self-sufficient and able to enjoy life to the full. I was now severely disabled with a Care Plan in place. In my past life, I had plans. In my present life, I was trying to come to terms with what I'd become, and living one day at a time. As for my future life, it was too scary to dwell on. But I knew I had to accept it. I was retiring in September and my working life would be over. It was six months since I'd last been at work and to be honest, it felt like a lifetime ago. But knowing that I'd never return, left me feeling bereft and empty. It was to be another massive change in my life, to add to all the other massive changes I'd experienced over the last six months.

Plans were made to take me home to assess my needs within my house, as an overnight stay was to be organised, to see how I got on.

Going home to my home for the first time, was very scary. I was taken home by Patient Transport, with Tracey and her colleague meeting me there. They had brought my gutter frame and freeway chair so that I could try them out in my house. When I arrived outside my home, the first thing I noticed was my garden being full of weeds and my hanging baskets full of dead flowers. When I'd left my home and been taken to hospital on the 28ᵗʰ of February, the baskets had been full of ivy and winter pansies.

Tracey and a colleague helped me up the steps and into my front door, as there was not yet a ramp for my wheelchair. I walked into my living room, using my gutter frame, where I then sat in my manual wheelchair. As it was not my electric one, I couldn't move it by myself, so had to just sit there, until someone moved me. I remember feeling totally detached from the home I'd loved and spent so much time renovating. Everything around me in the room was out of my reach and I felt so useless. It was noted that the couch was too low and would need to be raised to allow me to sit on it as I wouldn't be able to get myself out of it at the hight it was. My bed was also too low and would need to be raised to allow me to transfer from my freeway chair onto the bed or vice versa. My freeway chair could access the toilet, but my electric wheelchair would not get through the door to my bedroom or the bathroom. I was also assessed as needing a bath chair and I would be shown how to transfer onto this at the hospital. I left my home after an hour, feeling no attachment to it. It was full of my possessions, but it wouldn't have bothered me, if I never saw them again. I couldn't understand how I felt this way, but my analysis of it now, is that I had recognised that my home was like looking at my past, a past I could no longer be part of and so to protect myself, I had detached myself from all that it represented.

I went home for an overnight stay the weekend before I was scheduled to leave the hospital, as I'd had to wait until my bed had been heightened. The Community OT met us at my house and she and Tracey tested out, if I could transfer between the freeway chair and the bed, when my prosthetic legs were off. I could. Tracey also showed the Community OT, how to put my legs on and the OT took pictures of each stage of the process to give to the care assistants who would care for me, so they could use them as a guide. I remember seeing my bare legs for the first time, in the mirror wardrobe door in my bedroom and seeing my stumps and how they looked for anyone looking at me. I could clearly see how I now looked. Tracey advised me not to look at them, as she could see it was upsetting me, but I knew I needed to get used to how I looked. This was the image that I would see every morning until I moved to my new home.

Being home highlighted how much my room in the hospital fitted my needs and how my own home didn't. I could only sit in my wheelchair when in the living room. When I was in bed, my legs were off, so I was trapped in my bedroom until the morning, with a commode being put at the side of my bed, in case I needed the toilet. The other option was to wake Emma and I didn't want to do that. My hospital bed had sheets on it, but at home, I had a duvet and it restricted my movement. Having only one arm and no feet, meant it was hard for me to turn over in bed and I would swing myself over, using my hips, which did take a lot of effort. The duvet restricted my ability to do this even more, therefore to achieve this, I had to kick my duvet off, having to try and untangle my legs from it first. I then had to swing myself over, before sitting up and trying to pull the duvet back over me, which was hard to achieve as my right hand was still sensitive and lacking in strength. All this effort meant I was wide awake at the end of this process. As I had to do this process two or three times during the night, I was shattered when it was time to get up in the morning. These restrictions when I'm in my bed are still ongoing, with my sleep pattern, still problematic, and leaving me feeling constantly tired. But, it's just routine to me now and I've learned to accept it for what it is.

The experience of staying overnight in my own house to prepare me for going home, did not make me feel excited and confident about my forthcoming discharge. In fact, it made me feel apprehensive, vulnerable and scared.

My medication for phantom pain was reduced at my request and was eventually stopped once I was in no pain at all. The daily Fragmin injections ceased as I was more mobile and so at less risk of blood clots. The blood samples that had been taken every two days, for the duration of my time in hospital, were also stopped. It felt weird to be medication free and for someone who had four amputated limbs, not requiring medication was amazing.

The date for my discharge, was scheduled for Friday the 24th August. Although I knew this day would come, the reality that it was approaching was so frightening. I didn't want to leave the security of the hospital, the place that had been my home for the last six months and the only place I had lived without my legs and arms.

One of my worries about going home, was how I would get up if I fell, especially as I was going to be in the house myself for periods of time. When I discussed this with Kerry, she agreed we'd have to address this, but she said her dilemma was how to get me down on the ground first. Kerry and Tracey arranged for Sean, Kim and Emma to come into the gym one afternoon and we all met there, in the hope that a method could be found to alleviate my fear of falling and not being able to get up. To get me down on the floor, I sat on the plinth bed, which was then lowered to its lowest point. I then slid off the bed, onto a stool, then onto a wooden block. However, my feet became stuck in the ridge of the foam mat, that had been put down on the floor, so that I wouldn't be sitting on a hard surface. As my legs were straight and there was no flexibiity in my prosthetics, I was stuck. Another physiotherapist was asked to assist and as I tried to move forward on the wooden block it flipped onto its side, causing me to hit the ground with a bump. But on the plus side, I was now down on the floor.

I shuffled along the mat and turned around to face the bed, the bed I now had to try and get back up on. Firstly, I tried to get onto all fours, whilst still wearing my prosthetic legs, but due to only having one full length arm and a partial hand, which couldn't lie flat, I was unable to achieve this. One of my prosthetic legs was taken off, as well as the Iceross, the foam mould and the socks, to see if that helped my balance, but I still couldn't do it. So, my second prosthetic leg was removed, plus the Iceross, foam mould and socks, but with no success. I could balance on my knees, but with a lot of concentration. Most of my lower legs and feet had been amputated, so there wasn't much for me to balance on. Anyway, kneeling against the bed, having only one long arm, I tried to pull myself up, using my elbows to push against the bed, but to no avail. I didn't have the strength to achieve that and ended up dangling from the bed. I must have looked funny from the rear, with my stumps dangling below me. It was then that Sean lifted me from under my arms and put me on the bed, stating that, that was the only way I would be able to get off the floor, if

I fell. He was right and I found accepting that difficult. It meant I would never feel safe, always aware that I couldn't afford to fall, as I wouldn't be able to get up. The bigger picture was, that if I did eventually manage to be confident to walk outside. I would always need someone with me, to help me if I fell. I felt deflated. It was a big blow. I had achieved so much by learning to walk again and I felt I'd failed at the last hurdle. Kerry and Tracey reassured me that it wasn't my fault, that it was due to not having my left arm, making it impossible for me to pull or push myself up. I knew what they were telling me was true, but I so wanted to achieve this and knowing that I never would, was upsetting.

It was then that Sean interrupted our conversation to say that if we turned around and looked on the floor, it looked like I'd been blown up by a bomb. When we turned around and saw pieces of my prosthetic legs strewn across the floor, it did look like a bombsight. But it brightened the mood, with us all laughing at the surreal scene in front of us.

Because I had been in a coma for eight days, I was referred to a group called INSPIRE. I attended every Thursday afternoon, for five weeks, with the first session taking place the day before I was to leave the hospital. One of the criteria for attending the group, was to have been discharged from hospital and be living at home, with rehabilitation in progress. I was still in hospital, but due to my impending discharge and as the next group was not due until February 2019, it was felt that I would benefit more by attending this one. In attendance were staff from ICU, including the doctors who looked after me, a pharmacist, a physiotherapist, a nutritionist, a psychologist and volunteers, who themselves in the past had been in a coma. There were also other agencies, who attended on various weeks, to give support and advice.

Attending the group allowed me to meet others who had been in a coma, with everyone having a different story to tell. I also gained knowledge on the effects of being in a coma, which helped me understand more about why I was feeling as I did. I felt lacking in energy and constantly tired yet didn't sleep well. I learned that this is normal for a coma victim, as whilst in a coma, you're not sleeping normally - you are deprived of sleep. 2% of muscle mass is lost every day you're in a coma. As I was in a coma for over a week, I had lost nearly 20% of my muscle mass.

At the group, I was able to talk to a psychologist for the first time. I explained to her how much I had desperately needed psychological support. I had experienced the most horrific experiences, where I felt so alone and helpless, and yet help was not available. I was aware I wouldn't be the only one in this situation, so I wasn't talking just for myself, but for everyone who found themselves in similar situations.

I enjoyed attending the group over the next five weeks and would recommend it to anyone that meets the criteria. I'm not sure if it runs at other hospitals, but the hope is, that it will continue to run at Kirkcaldy Victoria Hospital, if funding is granted. I have nothing but praise for the ICU staff and the rest of the INSPIRE team, who are dedicated to organising and facilitating the group. They recognise it is so beneficial to people like myself, who need to know what happened to them and of the journey they face when they wake up from being in a coma.

On the week of my discharge I went with Kim and Emma to ICU and HDU with a thank you card and chocolates. Although it had been back in March that I had been a patient in these units, I needed to thank them for all the care they had given me. I knew I had been critically ill when these amazing people had looked after me and I needed to let them know how much I appreciated their dedication and care.

Saying thank you to the staff on Ward 33, and Kerry and Tracey in particular, required more than a box of chocolates. They had been with me every step of the way, throughout my gruelling journey, helping me remain strong and giving me the courage to keep going, even when at times, I wanted to give up. They made me feel safe, being by my side, celebrating every achievement I made and although my stay in Ward 33 had not been easy at times, they had helped me laugh again. I had so many memories of times full of laughter, with jokes, mostly aimed at me, being a daily occurrence. My family and friends also recognised how amazing they were, as they were welcomed and supported by them too. They often commented on this, appreciating how comfortable they were made to feel.

I wanted to show everyone of them - the doctors, nurses, nursing assistants, clerical staff, domestics and other individuals I haven't mentioned - how much I appreciated everything they had done for me. So, with the help of my sister Dianne and my friends, gifts for them all were purchased, along with a thank you card with a personal message from me printed out and pasted in it by my friend. Writing so many words was still too hard for me. The gifts I chose for them all, was a small bottle of Prosecco, with the label on it saying 'A Great Big Thank you from Marguerite', and a bag of homemade tablet. Knowing them all so well, I knew they would appreciate the booze, but I also knew they liked their sweets.

*

I bought a personal present for the male nurse I had met on my first night in Ward 33. He had shown me so much care during my time in the ward. He'd come up to HDU after he'd worked a nightshift, to make sure I was alright. (I had been taken there when my health deteriorated after I'd had my arms amputated). He had also contacted Ninewells to inquire how I was when I had been admitted to have my legs amputated. I don't think he realises how much that meant to me and how it helped me remain strong. At both these times, I felt I was living in a nightmare. I was so lonely and confused and knowing people out there cared, really helped me cope.

We had been through some journey as nurse and patient. He always recognised when I was feeling a bit low, even when I tried to hide it, as I usually did. He helped me regain my positive attitude, without even knowing. We both had a warped sense of humour and we had so many laughs together, usually at my expense. But it so helped me to cope and remain positive and strong. I was going to miss our chats about putting the world to right, in a warped and ridiculous way, with our silly ideas.

He would not be on duty, the morning I was to go home, so I gave him his gift earlier. It was emotional saying thank you and goodbye, as it made my going home real. But I remained strong. I had to be, as the alternative was to give in to how I was really feeling and I couldn't afford to do that. Because if I did, I knew I would never cope.

CHAPTER 15

Time to Go Home

Friday the 24th of August arrived. I hadn't slept well, but again, I never did. The night staff got me in the shower, as I had to be ready early, as the ambulance to take me home, could arrive at any time. My gifts for the staff had been brought in the night before by my friends so I asked one of the night staff to distribute them for me; I knew they would all be gathered for the handover and shift change. When she returned to thank me, she said, "Marguerite, please promise me that you'll do something with your life and not give up. You have not lost your brain and memory, and have so much to give to the world yet".

I was dressed and ready to go, with Kim and Emma having taken most of my possessions home the day before. I only had my suitcase and bits and bobs left to go home with me. My breakfast arrived, as did Kerry, to deliver her last ever morning coffee for me. We both tried to be upbeat, but I knew she was struggling emotionally, just like me. She had been with me from day one, even when I had been in a coma and I hadn't known she was there. She had been my rock throughout my journey and I was going to miss seeing her every day, keeping me strong. I'd never thought that I would walk again, when my legs were amputated, but she had believed in me and helped me achieve being able to stand on my own and walk on my own. For that, she will always have a special place in my heart. She told me months later, that at first, she had thought that I'd never be able to walk, but that idea had soon changed, when she began to work with me. She recognised the person I was - strong, committed and determined to achieve all I could be.

I gave Kerry her thank you present and card while we were on our own together. She told me she would open it later and I understood why. She knew my card was to be read when she was on her own.

Tracey arrived soon afterwards and opened her present and card, with a few tears flowing as we hugged. She, like Kerry, had been with me throughout my journey and had been committed to helping me be as independent as possible, sourcing gadgets and equipment, especially for me. She had been a great support in helping Sean make the building of my new home become a reality and had been there to give support to Kim and Emma when they needed it. Nothing was too much effort for Tracey. She went the extra mile on many occasions. She is a fantastic occupational therapist and someone I am privileged to have had looking after me during my long spell in hospital.

A stream of people visited me that morning to say goodbye and wish me good luck - the doctors who looked after me, the two phlebotomists, that had taken my blood every two days for nearly six months, along with various other staff that had been with me throughout my journey.

I found containing my emotions difficult when the ambulance crew finally arrived to take me home. Kerry arrived to take my suitcase, as she had arranged to come home with me. She wanted to make sure I was going to be alright. As I looked around my room, which was now bare and looked as if I'd never been in it, I took a deep breath and headed for the door. Kerry walked in front of me, pulling my suitcase behind her. The staff of Ward 33 were all waiting outside my room to say goodbye and on seeing them, I reversed back through the doorway, trying to hold back the tears, but I couldn't. When I emerged from my room for a second time, I wasn't the only one who was emotional. Some of the staff were wiping their eyes with their hankies too. By the time I had given them all a hug and said goodbye, I was in bits. Kerry had walked away in front and I knew she was finding keeping it together hard too.

Most people can't wait to leave hospital, but I'd have been happy to remain in the place I now saw as my home, where I felt safe and surrounded by the staff, who now knew me so well and who I now regarded as my friends. Being in hospital and the journey that entailed, had changed me forever and not just the way I looked. I recognised that

I was leaving behind, the kind of people I wanted to be surrounded by - caring, supportive, trustworthy, loyal and fun to be around and who knew the person I was now. Leaving them behind to face the world outside Ward 33, was scary, but I made my way to the exit door, took a deep breath, turning one last time to wave to them all and headed out of the ward. My time in Ward 33 was over, but my memories of my time there will remain with me forever. I had been in hospital for 177 days and I was going home to face reality. My life as it would be for me now, living without my arms and legs.

One of the ambulance crew said to me, en route to the ambulance, that he had never seen anyone leave the hospital with the send-off that I had received from the staff. They were all there to say goodbye. He said that I must have made some impression on them all. My reply to him was that they had made some impression on me.

I was quiet on the journey home, deep in my own thoughts. I felt I was re-entering the world I had left behind six months ago, and I didn't feel part of it anymore. My life on the outside world was going to be so different from what it had been before.

Kerry and Tracey arrived at my house at the same time as I did, having brought my gutter frame, freeway chair and my bath seat with them. Outside railings had been fitted on each side of the steps at my front door and I managed to climb the three steps into my house, with Kerry and Tracey's help. I walked into my living room, using my gutter frame. There in the room was a huge bunch of sunflowers from my friend, a welcome home gift. It would be the first of many bunches of flowers I would receive over the next few weeks. When I was given flowers in the past, I'd arrange them in a vase myself, but now I couldn't do that. I found it difficult to ask the people who had brought me the flowers to do this for me, so they often lay on the worktop waiting until Emma got home. In time, I did get better at asking for help and eventually, I was able to do this task on my own, only much, much further down the line and only if I used a vase that was not too heavy for me to handle.

As my NHS electric wheelchair was too heavy to be lifted into my house, it was parked in the garage. My manual wheelchair was wheeled into the living room for me to sit on.

Anyway, Kerry and Tracey made sure my bath seat and freeway chair were in the bathroom. I needed the freeway chair over the toilet, as I didn't have a disabled toilet in my home.

The Community OT, who would take over my care, also arrived and informed me that a care assistant would visit me the next morning to help me get out of bed and get dressed. She had a folder with her that the care assistant would complete each morning, as a daily update. The folder also contained the photographs that she had taken previously, which would give the staff pictorial instructions on the process of fitting my prosthetic legs.

My brother and sister-in-law, who live nearby, arrived with lunch and it was then time for me to say goodbye to Kerry and Tracey, with them giving me a hug and good luck wishes. Before leaving, Kerry told me that my home was just as she had envisaged it would be and she felt happy to leave me, knowing it would provide me with my basic needs until I moved into my new purpose-built home. I continued to see Kerry for physio twice a week, on Tuesday and Thursday mornings. I must admit that did help me cope at the time, knowing there was still that link with Kerry and the hospital.

Having lunch with my brother and sister-in-law, in my own house, felt strange. For the rest of the day, I was never on my own. My family made sure that I had plenty of company to help me settle in. As it was a Friday night, my friends arrived with a takeaway and I had a glass of wine to celebrate.

It was the start of me learning new routines too. At the hospital, the toilet was in my room, whereas now, I had to walk from the living-room to the bathroom at the end of the hall. This took a lot of effort, as the frame just fitted through the doors. Negotiating it into the bathroom wasn't easy.

At bedtime, brushing my teeth was another challenge. I'd always been in my freeway chair to brush them at the sink, but there was not enough space in my bathroom to do that. So I sat on the edge of the bath to clean my teeth, which was quite a challenge. I also had to bend down under the sink to get my toothbrush and toothpaste, a movement that required a lot of concentration as I bent forward. It was scary at first, but I mastered this quickly.

That night, Emma brought my freeway chair from the bathroom into the bedroom and placed it against my bed. A bedpan was attached to it, just in case I needed the toilet during the night. I had also been given a trolley, to enable me to transport things on. It was also put next to my bed, so my mobile phone and i-Pad were handy.

Emma helped me get undressed, before taking off my legs. But then the tears came. I couldn't help it. I thought "What has my life become?" My nineteen-year-old daughter was having to get her fifty-five-year-old mum ready for bed. It just wasn't right.

The furniture in my room had been moved around to allow more space for me to manoeuvre my chair, so the room didn't feel like mine anymore. As I lay there in the dark, feeling so frightened of the life that lay ahead for me, I so wanted to be back in the hospital where I felt safe.

A key box had been put on the wall in the back garden of my home to allow carers to access a key to enable them to open my front door and get into the house. So, the next morning, Saturday the 25th of August, I heard the key open the door and the carer coming in. She was a stranger to me and I felt awkward, but she was very caring and probably as nervous as I was. I knew she would not have worked with someone like me, a quadruple amputee and so I would have to explain to her my morning routine, making her aware of what I could do myself and what I needed help with.

I could not access the shower cubicle in my bathroom and had been given a bath seat from the hospital. However, I would not get a bath in the mornings, as the carers were not allowed to bath me, due to the health and safety risks the seat in the bath posed. This was because I had to transfer from the freeway chair onto the bath seat, by sliding onto it. As I had no legs, I was at risk of losing my balance, which would lead to me falling forward and banging my head on the bath taps. At first, the plan was that I'd receive a bed bath until my new home was built, but my good balance and ability to transfer capably, meant Tracey had agreed to allow Kim and Emma to give me a bath and this would take place in the evenings, when they were around.

Back to my first visit from the carer, which would become an every day visit for months to come, until a Care Package was assessed by Social

Work. The carer held my freeway chair against my bed as instructed, which I wriggled onto before being wheeled into the bathroom. I needed help to squeeze the water out of my facecloth and with washing the right side of my body, due to having no left hand. Then it was back into the bedroom, to wriggle back onto the bed, where I needed help to dress and put my deodorant on. Another task, I couldn't do and still can't achieve. I then explained to her, the process of putting on my prosthetic legs. Although the photos were in the folder to help, it was easier for me to explain how they went together. She was worried that she was going to hurt me and was apprehensive, but she managed to get them on and I stood up, using my gutter frame to get them to click into place securely, with me rocking from one foot to the other, until the clicks stopped. She could then put my trousers on and I then walked to the drawer to get my brush, brush my hair and put moisturiser on my face, with me having learned to open the jar, by holding it in my stump.

She then made me a cup of coffee and some toast, before filling in the folder. And then I was left in the house on my own, as Emma was at her work. This was the first time I'd ever been alone, since going into hospital and it felt strange and scary. It seems strange to say, but I felt vulnerable in my own home and couldn't stop thinking, that I just wanted to go back to the hospital, to Ward 33, where I felt safe.

CHAPTER 16

ROCKORE

That Saturday, the local Music Festival, Rockore, took place and my friend had encouraged me to go along with her and her family. I had mixed emotions about attending. There would be lots of people there and I didn't know if I could handle that. I was already feeling vulnerable, being in the house myself, so how would I cope at a busy venue, with hundreds of people there? Would I manage to go to the toilet, on a portaloo?

My friend Helen phoned me, asking if I was up to going and I remember gabbling on about how disorientated I was feeling in my own home and my worries of attending the festival. She convinced me to give it a go, stating that she would bring me home if it became too much for me. She arranged to come to my house and help me get ready and her support helped calm my nerves, even though she now recalls being more of a hindrance than a help.

She put her bag on the floor in the hallway, when she arrived, causing an obstruction right away. She must have moved her bag two or three times, always putting it on the floor, before the penny dropped, to put it on the chair. Her actions made me laugh, easing my anxiety, but raising hers. She then looked at my feet and asked me if I'd be better with shoes on, instead of sandals, as my feet might get cold. As soon as she said it, she realised the obvious. My feet weren't real. Her face was a picture! How we both laughed. She's not the only one who forgot my legs and feet aren't real and made similar remarks. I'm sure similar situations will occur in the future, with no malice or upset intended, and I will laugh them off as well. It's the only way to approach it.

Anyway, back to the story. Her husband Patrick turned up to help and got my NHS electric wheelchair out of my garage, with me having to go down the two steps at the front door to access it. Stepping down the two steps was scary and my friend stayed behind me, holding my hood, whilst her husband helped me from the front. We all laughed at how little help holding my hood would have been, if I had fallen. The reality was, that like most people, knowing what to do to help me was difficult. My family and friends were having to learn how to support a quadruple amputee, with complex needs, and it would take time for them to become skilled in what these needs were. These needs would also continue to change as my mobility improved.

Attending Rockore was the best thing I could have done that day. Yes, being amidst thousands of people was daunting, but whilst there, I could forget about being home and the next stage of my journey. Lots of people came over to see me, many I didn't even know, to give me a hug and words of encouragement, and although having to attend the festival in a wheelchair was challenging for me, I didn't feel vulnerable. I felt safe amongst people from my community, who had shown me so much support over the last six months. Many sent me cards and messages during my stay in hospital, as well as organising or supporting

Figure 23; Rockore 2018

all the fundraising events. Over the years, I have attended many Benarty Fundraising Events with Kim and Emma - from the Gala Day, the Ghost Walk, the Santa Parade, and the Pipe Band Competition – but, Rockore 2018 will always remain a special event to me.

I worried that I would be unable to use the disabled portaloo, but I managed to accomplish this without difficulty. It was a major achievement for me. I began to recognise that I could challenge my fears and succeed.

At the festival, I drank wine from the plastic wine glass that I had taken with me. I could hold the wine glass by the stem, but was unable to hold the plastic tumblers that drink was being served in. I remember sipping my wine and talking to Patrick about how vulnerable and frightening it was now that I was back home. His response will stay with me forever. It reminded me how near to death I had been and how far I had come. He said; "Marguerite, six months ago, I came into ICU to say goodbye to you, so the fact that we're sitting here today, having a drink together, never mind, what you have managed to achieve over the last six months, is nothing short of a miracle."

On returning home from Rockore, my friends helped get me ready for bed and take my legs off, as Emma was out with her friends. They then left, locking the door behind them. A year later, I would attend Rockore again, but on returning home this time, I did not need help. I said goodbye at the front door and got ready for bed myself.

CHAPTER 17

Reality Hits Home

Sunday, the day after I attended Rockore, my sister and brother-in-law came to visit, bringing lunch. It was a weird feeling, seeing her in my kitchen, preparing food, the kitchen I had never used, with it just having been fitted just before I'd become unwell. I felt so helpless and useless. I had always been the one in the kitchen, the hostess with the mostest, and it was hard not being able to be that anymore. It emphasised yet another part of who I had been before, that no longer existed. But I did manage, with a struggle, to get into the kitchen in my wheelchair and sit at the table, which felt good.

Emma had been working all day, but arrived home after my visitors had left and we had a take away for tea. We discussed ideas for easy meals she could cook over the next few days. However, we needn't have worried about meals, as it soon became apparent, that our family and friends would provide them in plenty. We always had something homemade and delicious to eat. It would be some time to come before I could use the microwave, or open tubs, as my hand was still weak and sensitive. I had to rely on Emma or others to do this for me.

I found the first week at home extremely difficult. In the hospital, I had felt I was as independent as I could be within the environment of my room, but home emphasised my new reality. I could do very little for myself. I couldn't wring the cloth out to wipe the work tops. I couldn't open the fridge door. I couldn't lift the kettle, so couldn't fill it with water, or pour water from it, so I couldn't even make myself a coffee. Taking lids off bottles, jars and tins was also too difficult, not just because my hand was sensitive and weak, but also because my limited hand span made it impossible.

By the Tuesday, I was struggling with my limitations and the frustrations this caused me, but I tried hard to remain positive. As I sat in my chair that day, I became aware of a pungent smell coming from the kitchen. I walked into the kitchen, using my gutter frame, and opened the cupboard door where the buckets were kept. Right away, I could tell that the smell was coming from the food waste bin. On opening it, I saw the source of the smell - the chicken carcass from the Sunday, when my sister had visited and made my lunch. As soon as I'd opened the bucket, the smell filled the room and I knew I had to try and empty it and get it outside. I knew I couldn't lift the brown bin, so I tried to lift the bin bag from it. However, on lifting the bag out of the bin, the bottom split, spilling the contents all over the floor. I stood there in the kitchen, surrounded by rotten food waste, with the smell beginning to overwhelm me. I was unable to bend down to pick it up. I couldn't even open the windows, to let fresh in air. All I could do was go and sit in my wheelchair and wait until someone came and cleared up the mess.

I sat in my chair and sobbed at the realisation that I couldn't even empty a bucket, without making more mess. My uncle arrived soon after and cleaned up the mess and opened the window for me. He then made me a cup of coffee, making sure I was alright, before he left.

Similar situations happened regularly, as I would continue to try and do tasks on my own, usually leading to creating more work for Emma when she got home from college. I knew I needed to keep trying to do things on my own, but it was hard going. And very frustrating. Tackling challenges seemed more difficult in the early days, as I think emotionally, I was struggling to accept the situation I found myself in and my body was still in the early stages of recovery. I was still quite weak and lacking in strength. Plus, my right hand was still healing and was tender and sensitive to the touch, making its usage limited.

I remember on one occasion, my friend came to visit and brought me a gift of a Chocolate Orange. She laid it on the coffee table and as I looked at it, I thought, "Why would she bring me that, when I couldn't hold it or open it, never mind break the chocolate leaves apart, to eat it?" I felt a bit upset that she could be so insensitive. I soon realised however, that she wouldn't have thought about me not being able to open it. Why would she? She was learning, just like me, how to cope with this alien world we found ourselves in, where nothing remained as it had been before and that was hard to comprehend and to get used to. So, I laughed and made a joke about her blunder and she laughed too, before opening the chocolate and breaking it into pieces for me. She left the chocolate segments for me in a bag that I could open later. There were many more occasions when people's lack of understanding of my restrictions created similar situations. Another example was being gifted scented candles, which I love. Previously, I lit one in my home on most evenings. Now however, I can no longer light them, so they are unusable. I've tried to source a lighter I can operate with my half thumb, but unfortunately, I've still not managed to find one.

I know I'll continue to come across obstacles every day which I have to problem-solve. It's now part of being me and I've learned to cope with that, although I admit, I sometimes can't help getting frustrated at times.

Arrangements were made for me to be collected from my home by Patient Transport, so that I could continue to attend my physiotherapy sessions with Kerry. These sessions would continue for many months to come, with me building relationships with many of the members of the ambulance crews.

Emma would get my wheelchair from the garage and left it at the front door, at the bottom of the steps, but on rainy days, the ambulance crew got it out of the garage for me. Although I found walking up and down stairs difficult, I became more confident at this as time went on.

I did struggle with using Patient Transport to begin with, as the other transport users tended to be elderly. I couldn't help thinking, "What's happened to me, what have I become?" The reality was that I was now severely disabled and could do very little for myself. I needed the same support at the age of fifty-five, that most of these elderly people needed. I was using this service at least twenty years earlier than I should have.

However, on the positive side, using Patient Transport, meant I could attend my physio sessions with Kerry and continue to build on strengthening my legs, my core, practise my walking and balancing skills, as well as using stairs more efficiently. It also meant I was back in the hospital, where I felt safe and surrounded by people who knew me for who I was now. As the physio department was next door to Ward 33, I'd pop into the ward along with Kerry, to see the staff and they were always pleased to see me, to give me a cuddle and enquire how I was getting on living at home. It was strange seeing another patient in my room, which the staff admitted to still calling, 'Marguerite's room'. I'd jokingly said, when still in hospital, that a plaque be put up outside the door naming it 'The Marguerite Henderson Suite'. On one occasion when I visited the ward, the room was having new flooring done and I suggested that a star with my name on it could be put on the floor, just like they have stars for celebrities on the pavement on Hollywood Boulevard. I so missed the banter with staff and how protective they were of me. They were like family to me now and I missed not seeing them every day.

Apart from doing my physio, I also was able to talk to Kerry about how life was at home and as she knew me so well that she knew how to encourage me and keep me motivated. I also continued to meet with Lynne on a Thursday and that continued for many months. She knew her support was essential.

I also attended the INSPIRE group on a Thursday afternoon for the next four weeks. As I've mentioned earlier in my story, this group was to support people who had been in a coma, helping them to have an understanding of the effects on their body whilst in the coma, and of living with the after-effects a coma can create. You could arrange to meet with the professionals in attendance to get advice or seek additional support. I was able to meet with a psychologist, which couldn't have come at a better time for me, when I was trying to adapt to living at home. By attending the group, you were also given a wide range of information regarding the support that was available and how to access it if needed.

When I attended the last session of the group, I was not in a good place. I was struggling on so many levels and talking to the psychologist was so needed that day. Finding out that psychological support was to continue helped me that day, as knowing the group meetings were coming to an end, had been a big worry for me.

I remember at one session sitting in my wheelchair, having a coffee, when one of the ICU consultants introduced me to the pharmacist who had been in attendance at every session, but who I had not had any dealings with as I was not taking any medication. The pharmacist told me that although I wouldn't remember him, I would be one of the patients he would remember throughout his career. He said that on Thursday, the 1st March, he had been contemplating heading home because of the heavy snow, when he had received a phone call from ICU, requesting his help. When he'd arrived in ICU, he said that the sight he'd encountered would remain with him forever. He had never seen so many doctors and medical staff around a patient's bed. That bed was mine. He was informed that the staff and my family had been told to prepare for the worst, as I was not responding to any treatment. The doctors had asked him if he had any suggestions, or knew of any other treatment they could try. He had suggested another drug, but gave no promises that it would work. The pharmacist told me that when he had entered ICU the next day, he hadn't expected to see me alive and still lying in the bed. But I was. The medication he had suggested had been successful and had saved my life.

I remember looking at him and saying, "So it's your fault I'm still alive?" and him asking me if I was joking or being serious. The consultant laughed, stating, that today, he didn't think I was joking. He was right, as that day, I was struggling to understand why I'd been allowed to live, as living everyday was so hard. Too hard at times. At these times, it was so scary to think of me living into my old age, as being as disabled as I was, I knew my mobility would more than likely deteriorate with age, making living without my arms and legs even harder.

Getting used to being at home was hard. The ICAS carer arrived every morning and once she'd left, I was often on my own, as Emma would be at college or at her work. The carers were all lovely and tried to let me know who would be coming in each morning. They seemed aware of how hard being at home was for me and how frustrated I became with my limitations. I also became aware of how intrusive their presence in the house was for Emma, but she never complained and actually built up relationships with them, just accepting them being there, as part of her daily routine as well as mine.

Being in the manual wheelchair meant I was less mobile and as my legs were now too big and therefore felt heavier to walk in, my mobility to get around was much harder. I sat there looking out of the patio doors at my garden, being unable to access outside either, until a raised patio and ramp was erected. I felt so alone.

I had to re-learn how to use the controls for the television and Sky, as I'd totally forgotten how to use them. If they fell on the floor, bending over to pick them up was difficult, as I used so much effort to balance and I became exhausted when I had to attempt this.

My family and friends made sure someone was there to give me lunch and tea, and Emma was there to put me to bed. Sometimes she went out with her friends after I was in bed, but she always made sure my commode was in place, even though she knew I had no intention of using it. I was aware friends and family were concerned about me being in the house at night on my own, but I needed to be able to do this. Plus, making Emma stay at home to be with me wasn't fair on her. For her to have that responsibility every night, restricting her of being able to go out and have fun, like every other eighteen year old, wasn't right and I needed to make sure that her life was as normal as it could be, under the circumstances she found herself in, through no fault of her own.

My Friday night, wine nights, continued and still do, although it's often gin night now. Before sepsis struck, our Friday nights were to celebrate it being the end of our working week and the start of the weekend. But that has changed, as it's now the night when my friends visit me, just for a weekly catch up.

During my first week at home, Emma and two of my friends went through all my clothes, shoes, bags and accessories, with me sitting on the bed choosing what to keep and what to donate to the charity shop. None of my shoes or boots were appropriate for me to keep. Most were too big for my prosthetic feet, or they had too much of a heel, or were too flat. Dresses I wore with thick tights, trousers with buttons, or slim fitting ones, long tops and cardigans, all had to go. Buttons were off limit. Tights or slim fitting trousers were unwearable on my prosthetic legs and too difficult for me to pull on and off. Long tops and cardigans were too restricting for me to wear, as they got in my way, when I went to the toilet. All my tights and most of my sock collection went, as did most of my underwear, as I now needed to wear bigger pants to enable me to pull them on and off. I now needed to wear sports bras to enable me to have more independence when getting ready for bed. Most of my bras were now surplus to requirement. However, I did keep all my pyjamas, as a friend agreed to make all my long pyjama trousers into cropped ones, to suit my amputated legs. If I'd have worn long trousers to bed, they would have wrapped around my stumps, restricting my movement.

Some of my coats were not suitable to wear when sitting in my wheelchair. My handbag collection dwindled to only a few, as I now could only use a small bag, one that was lightweight and could be put over my shoulder allowing me easy access when sitting in my wheelchair. Gloves for obvious reasons were no use to me anymore and long scarves were too much of a hindrance. As for jewellery, long necklaces were no use, as they got in my way. But I refused to get rid of my large collection of jewellery, that I'd loved wearing daily. I kept all my jewellery, even though I was unable to put it on by myself. But most pieces had been given to me as gifts and so had sentimental value to me. I could not part with them.

By the end of the task, my wardrobe and two chests of drawers were mostly empty, with numerous black bags full of my possessions, piled up to go to the charity shop. It was distressing for me, as it emphasised how my wardrobe now focussed on the practicality of the items I could wear, rather than, what I would have chosen to wear and what had made me, ME. It highlighted yet another loss - who I had been before sepsis had taken everything that had represented me away from me. It felt like someone had erased me from the neck down, rubbing out my previous life and the person I had been before with it. I didn't know who I was anymore and didn't know if I would be able to find me again, or if I even wanted to. All I knew, was that I was still me from the neck up and as I hadn't been fully erased. I had no choice but to take one day at a time, build a new me, whoever that turned out to be.

Also, during my first week home, I ventured to the local shops, with support. Venturing out into the community was daunting for me, as the last time I had been at the local shops, was Saturday the 24th February, before I fell ill. It felt like a lifetime away. I also felt vulnerable at being outside, in the street. I knew people would stare at my deformities and I still found this hard to cope with and still do. I was told once by someone, that when I see people stare from car windows, or when walking by me, that I am not to assume they are looking at me for how I look, but that they are looking at me with admiration. I remind myself of her words, when I feel people staring. Although I am well aware that most of them are probably looking at me due to how disabled I look, some may be looking at me with admiration and it does help me feel better.

On the way to the local shops, finding dips in the pavements to enable me to cross the roads was problematic, as was the height of the kerbs, having to go down some backwards. I was frightened that my wheelchair would tip.

The first shop I came to was the bakers and although it had been recently refurbished, they had not thought to make the entrance to the shop accessible to wheelchairs, so I couldn't get in. The Chemist did have a ramp, but had a step at the top of it, so I was unable to go in. Even if I had been able to get in, it was too small to accommodate my chair. The next shop, yet again, was inaccessible, due to the width of the aisles. As there was a step into the shop that came next, I could not access it either. It turned out that the only shops in the street I could access, were the butchers and the Co-op.

However, it was nice to choose my own food and the outing was better than I'd imagined it would be. Many people stopped to ask how I was, ask how the building of my new home was progressing, and to give me words of praise and encouragement. Many people tell me I'm an inspiration but I don't see myself as that. In fact, I've come to dislike the word, as its not me. I'm just Marguerite, who is trying hard to make the most of what has happened to her.

On the 1st September I attended a second fundraising event for 'Music for Marguerite'. It took place in a Dunfermline pub and I attended along with a few of my close friends. Although I was apprehensive about attending the event in a pub, as I hadn't been in a pub in my wheelchair, up until then and I knew there would be a lot of young people there, as bands would be playing, I was glad I went. They were so pleased I was there and recognising how so many people had gone to so much effort to make the event a success, for me, was so humbling and I was truly grateful. Apart from that, I had a really nice time.

I became officially retired on the 7th September and I remember feeling so sad. It didn't feel real. I didn't have a last day at work, a speech from management, good luck wishes from colleagues, a retirement card or present, nothing. A colleague did contact me at a later date, to ask what I'd like to do to mark the occasion. I told her I didn't know, as my retiral wasn't one to celebrate. I'd not seen most of my colleagues since that awkward visit to my place of work in May and I knew I couldn't cope with seeing them all, happy and getting along fine with their own busy lives. How would I be perceived by them now? However, I did agree to meet up with the people that I still saw regularly, but that never happened.

I can't deny being upset and disappointed when I look back on this milestone, marking the end of thirty-five years' service with Fife Council. I was forced to retire early because of horrific, life-changing circumstances. Yet my retiral was totally disregarded by management and my colleagues. I can't help feeling upset, and so disappointed. It feels as if the hundred percent commitment I gave to my work and the relationship I thought I had with my colleagues, meant nothing. I have spent many sleepless nights worrying and trying to make sense of it all, with it having a massive impact on my health and well-being. I have a Memory Box for the year 2018 and I have no get well card or retirement card from my work. I have individual ones from some colleagues and I do appreciate them, but having get well cards from other teams in Fife Council only emphasises the lack of one from my own team and it really hurts. Although I've tried to move on and forget about it, with the help of my psychologist, every time I read on social media about someone else leaving the team, expressing their thanks for gifts and cards, I can't help getting upset and asking myself why I was forgotten about. Instead of feeling a sense of pride and achievement, I now feel my working life meant nothing and my contribution meant nothing. I do hope these feelings change, as I know it continues to have an impact on my emotional well-being and hinders my ability to remain positive about who I am as a person.

Having retired, I needed to attend an appointment at the Job Centre to discuss the extent of my disabilities and how it affected my ability to work. I had spent hours on the phone, frustrated at trying to arrange an appointment time and request the paperwork I needed to complete, to take to the appointment with me. I'd never had to access a Job Centre before and having to be taken there in my wheelchair, made it even more humiliating. However, the girl that I met with, when she saw me, was very supportive and understood how difficult attending the appointment was for me. She acknowledged how recently I had sustained my amputations and how the severity of my condition rendered me unable to work. Even getting to a place of work would be too problematic, as I needed to be chauffeured everywhere and without yet having a vehicle able to take my electric wheelchair, I needed someone to push me in my manual wheelchair wherever I went.

I hadn't realised that I should have brought a doctor's certificate, and agreed to request one and post it to her. My first line was for two months, which seemed ludicrous, considering my situation. My disabilities were not going to get better in two months and due to my lack of mobility, I needed someone to collect the line from the surgery and then post it. However, my second line was for six months and Emma sent it on-line, using my phone, making it a much simpler task. Thereafter, I was excluded from needing to produce a sick line, as my condition was considered long term and I was so grateful for this. I found the whole scenario of having to claim benefits stressful and arranging to get sick lines collected and sent on line added to my anxiety.

*

Earlier in my story, I spoke about being assessed for an electric wheelchair at The Astley Ainslie Hospital in Edinburgh. I needed an extending chair but NHS Fife did not provide them. My brother applied to The Mary Leishman Foundation for funding and happily his application was successful. That chair arrived around the middle of September. Getting it into the house was a struggle, as although French doors had been fitted to replace the patio doors, the raised patio and ramp, had still to be completed. Once in, it replaced my manual chair in the living-room, but as it was a tight fit for it to get through the doorways to access the kitchen, hall or my bedroom and too big to enter the bathroom with, I tended to keep it in the living-room. If I did take it into the kitchen to sit at the table to eat, there was a risk of it damaging the kitchen units, so I refrained from doing this on a regular basis. Being unable to access most areas of the house in my chair meant that I continued to use my gutter frame to walk and access the other rooms in my home.

I received my second pair of legs in September, due to my legs having shrunk, which is part of the normal healing process, but it was the start of a long drawn out saga, of ill fitted legs, that ultimately had a massive effect on my ability to walk confidently. Kerry noticed right away, when I went for physio, that my right leg was squint and contacted Ninewells to discuss this with them. When I received my legs, I hadn't noticed it, but I'd soon learn, that on putting new legs on, you don't know how they really are going to be, until you wear them for a time.

It soon become apparent, that my right prosthetic leg made me walk with my leg bent inwards and this got worse as time went on. Kerry was unable to continue my progress in practicing walking up flights of stairs and going up and down slopes. She felt it was too dangerous. So, she concentrated on building up the strength in my legs, which was necessary to improve my balance.

CHAPTER 18

Life at Home

October arrived and the building of the patio and ramp outside the French doors was completed. But the weather had changed and it became more difficult for me to get out. However, it made life so much easier for me when I did venture out, as I could now get in and out of the house, using my electric wheelchair.

The dark nights had well and truly arrived and I was beginning to feel that I was living in a prison cell. I did get lots of visitors, but I was stuck indoors. I couldn't help thinking about how my life had been before, when I had arms and legs. Back then I was in control of my own life, could drive, could go where ever I liked, whenever I liked. I now felt like I had no control and had to rely on others. Every day the realisation of how much help I needed was reiterated. Many of the everyday tasks I tried to achieve now proved too difficult for me.

I knew I had to remain positive and focussed for my own sanity, so I tried really hard to keep accomplishing small tasks. My friends, Mary and Raymond brought me a One Cup Kettle one day. It was brilliant. It enabled me to make myself a coffee. But only if the lid on the coffee jar was not screwed on tightly. If it was, I couldn't open it with my hand being sensitive and weak. I could also heat up food in the microwave if it was in a light-weight dish, as I could slide it out of the microwave onto the work top, without having to lift it. Using the oven was not possible, as my oven was underneath my hob. I could not bend down to put food in or out of it. I also couldn't lift the oven trays out and up onto the worktop and if the dish containing the food was too heavy, it was impossible for me to lift it up.

Any food I heated up, I had to be able to eat with a fork or spoon, as I couldn't use a knife to cut my food up. I soon recognised that my weekly diet consisted of, soup or a filled roll or sandwich for lunch, with the roll or sandwich being prepared for me, with it having to be not too big for me to hold and with not too much filling added, as having no fingers and a minimal grasp to hold them, the filling would easily fall out. My main meals consisted of fish, mince dishes, stews, curry and pasta. Spaghetti and tagliatelle had to be cut into smaller pieces to enable me to eat it.

My diet has not changed over the months as I cannot hold a knife. But at times I can't resist having other foods. When that happens, the food needs to be cut up into small pieces for me, but that makes the appearance of my plate less appetising.

As I could no longer do my own house work, someone came to do a weekly clean for me, but I also tried do some house-hold chores by myself. I dusted using a feather duster and used multi-purpose wipes to wipe the kitchen worktops, or clean the bathroom, although I couldn't clean the shower cubicle or bath, as they were too low for me to reach into. I gave up trying to hoover. It was too dangerous, as I could so easily trip over the cable. However, sometime later, my big sister Dianne bought me a cordless hoover, which would alleviate this issue. Purchasing a hoover that would suit my needs entailed a lot of research, as it needed to be light weight and have an on/off switch I was able to operate. Buying on line, or from a catalogue was out of the question, as I had to try it out, to see if it was suitable. Eventually, I did find one and although, it hasn't the strongest of suction, it's adequate for my needs. Being lightweight meant that I could hold it and balance for a short time on my legs, in order to use it. I could also use it, whilst in my wheelchair and hold it between my legs, whilst I hoovered the floor.

The building of my new home was well on the way and taking shape. As it was being built on the side of Sean and Kim's home, I could witness the impact it had on their everyday life. They had to enter their home through the extension, which meant walking along batons of wood, to get to their front door. Erin and Gracie no longer had their garden to play in as it was too dangerous for them to be in it. They were all living in a building site and it reinforced to me how committed they were to making me a new home, no matter how it affected them. I could not be prouder of them.

*

My ability to remain strong was being challenged beyond belief. I could have so easily opted to stay in my bed every day, but knew that would be my downfall. So, I got up when the carers arrived and got my legs on, even though I knew the day ahead would bring challenges. Knowing that made me feel deflated and lacking in enthusiasm.

I was struggling with sitting twenty-four seven, in a house that I no longer felt safe in, as it was no longer adequate for my needs. Everything around me reminded me of how different my life was, to the one I'd planned. My house had been renovated for my future, the future I would no longer see, and sitting in it daily reiterated what I'd lost. I had loved putting my stamp on each room, choosing the décor and decorating it myself with love. Now the feeling of attachment to my home had gone and I knew it would never return. It didn't provide the home I now required, making my life worth living, and it was slowly sucking the life out of me.

I was invited to attend The Murray Foundation Group at the hospital, which was a support group for amputees. I sat in my electric wheelchair, listening to attendees talking about the issues they faced daily, after losing their limbs. All I could think of, was that I wished I had only lost one leg, or even two legs, never mind having lost my arms too. I felt I didn't fit in, or belonged, as no one else in the group was coping with living without all four limbs being affected by amputation and so couldn't possibly understand how I felt. But the reality was, that there wasn't a group for people similar to myself, as the situation I found myself in was so rare.

I had been told often by physio and OT staff that other amputees who had seen me in the gym, had told them that I'd given them the inspiration to walk again, after watching me achieve walking and it did highlight how I was perceived by others. I should have been proud of myself, but instead, due to feeling low at that time, all I could think of was that I had nobody to get inspiration from and I needed to have that so badly.

A psychologist now visited me at home, as I didn't feel comfortable going to meet with her at her clinic. She also recognised how hard it was for me to remain in a house that emphasised what I'd lost and was so inadequate for my daily needs. Her support helped give me the ability to focus on moving to my new house, where my future would be. That would be a few months yet, but I knew it would happen and that kept me on track.

I received my prosthetic arm at the end of October. It was very heavy and seemed so much longer than my real arm had been, even though it wasn't. As my right hand had no fingers, it was hard to replica how my hand had looked. I was able to tell them that I'd had long piano fingers, like my dad's had been, with my nails always manicured and varnished. Although Kim's hands were different to what mine had looked like, she had long fingers too, so my prosthetist decided to use her hand as the model for my prosthetic arm.

The arm consisted of an Iceross, which was put on my arm and then the prosthetic arm would click onto it. It was different from my legs, as I could put it on and take it off by myself. This was necessary to allow me to remove it when I went to the toilet. It was only for cosmetic use and had no pliability or function. In fact, it often just got in the way. However, wearing it helped stop the stares from people, when they noticed I had no arm and that was a bonus. It helped my confidence when out in public.

The first time I wore my arm in public, I was going to my physio session with Kerry at the hospital. I was in the lift, sitting in my electric wheelchair, along with five members of the public and two physiotherapists, one of whom I knew very well, as she was a friend of Kerry's. I remember thinking that no one was looking at me and how good that felt, when Kerry's friend suddenly noticed I had my arm and said, "Marguerite, you've got your arm! It looks real!", turning to the other physio and stating, "Doesn't it look real?" My cover was blown, as everyone on the lift automatically looked at my arm. When we got off the lift, I thanked her for blowing my cover and she was mortified at her blunder. I saw the funny side of it and we have both laughed about what happened since. I do think that it happening whilst I was in the hospital helped, as I felt less vulnerable and safe there.

However, it was hard seeing my prosthetic arm lying at the bottom of my bed at night, along with my two prosthetic legs. They represented my missing limbs. It really did highlight the enormity of the situation I now found myself in and that was so scary. I, would be lying in my bed, staring at my missing lower legs, feet, arm and hand and my heart would begin to pound in panic. It was if I

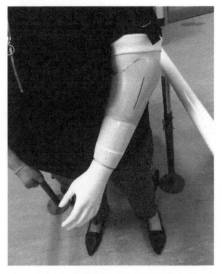

Figure 24; My Prosthetic Arm, without it's skin

hadn't noticed I had missing limbs before and I was seeing what I now looked like for the first time. This anxiety episode happened regularly and I now think that was as a result of reality kicking in.

My granddaughters Erin and Gracie helped me cope with the enormity of it all, as they just accepted me as I was. Erin would help me take my prosthetic limbs, not at all inhibited by what it represented. As for Gracie, she would try to help too, but really preferred to play

Figure 25; My Prosthetic Arm, with its skin on

with them and try to put them on. I remember on one occasion my friend visiting and Gracie putting my arm on and singing the song 'Baby Shark', whilst doing the actions, using my arm. It was a surreal situation, but so funny.

November came and I outgrew my gutter frame. I now used my trolley as a means of support around the house and to carry my mobile. I needed to carry my mobile with me at all times, in case I needed to call someone for help. However, I also began to use a walking-stick and used that when outside, walking to the car.

By the end of the month, I would wheel my freeway chair through to my bedroom at bedtime, but still refrained if I could, from using it as a commode during the night. As I needed my trolley by my bedside too, I would push it with the chair, like a train. Once sitting on the bed, I could also now take my own legs off by pressing the release button on each leg with my half thumb and shaking them until they came off. The left leg was harder to get off, as the button was on the left-hand side of it, so harder for me to reach, but perseverance paid off. Achieving all of these skills meant I was fully independent at bedtime and although my bedtime routine took me a while to complete and left me exhausted, I felt a sense of achievement and power, being totally independent of needing help. It felt good.

I also continued to achieve other skills and even if they were simple everyday tasks, they were massive achievements to me. I could now empty the dishwasher and put the dishes back in the cupboard. I would put the dishes in the cupboard one at a time, as more than one, meant they were too heavy for me to lift.

I began to open my own mail, using a letter opener. Holding and pulling the knife along the inside of the envelope seal took all the strength I could muster in my hand, but I got better and better at it. I was also getting better at writing. My signature was never the same twice, but what did that matter, was that I was able to hold a pen and control its movements.

I was also now able to pick up smaller items, even by bending over and picking them off the floor, using my half thumb and stubs, in a pincer grasp.

The weather became colder, the days being shorter, meaning that each day indoors felt like two days. The deterioration in the weather meant getting out was more difficult and when I did go out, I had begun to notice that my right hand went blue in colour if it got cold. My sister-in-law Linda, kindly knitted me a mitten that fitted snuggly on my finger-less hand and half thumb. It was just the thing to keep my hand cosy, and still allowed me to use the control on my wheelchair.

My ill-fitting right leg continued to affect my walking, so it was back to Ninewells to have it re-cast. It took two or three weeks for it to be made, but I was happy that I was going to receive another leg and I could get back to focussing on improving my walking ability.

In November, Erin's annual Dance Show took place. I had been to it the previous year and did not want to miss attending it this year. I wanted to get there early to avoid the last-minute crowds, as I hated everyone towering above me, whilst sitting in my wheelchair. However, things didn't go according to plan. Firstly, Emma was still learning about the appropriate timescales needed when dealing with me. I couldn't be rushed but she didn't give herself enough time to get me ready and arrive there in time. It was also raining heavily and was dark outside, so it was scary just getting out of the house and down the front door steps. Walking in the dark to the car, I nearly opted out of going. But anyway, I did walk to the car with Emma's help and her holding an umbrella over us to keep us dry. The rain was torrential when we reached the venue. We parked at the back of the building as there was no disabled spaces left. Emma got my wheelchair out of the boot and got it ready for me to sit in. Unfortunately, the heavy rain meant the seat became wet, so when I sat in it, my bottom became wet too. Emma tried her best to hurry and get me out of the rain, running across the car park and pushing my chair, whilst holding an umbrella at the same time. All of a sudden, my wheel-chair jerked me forward. We had gone through a pothole in the middle of a puddle. As I was jerked forward, the bunch of roses I had brought as a gift for Erin, flew out of my hand and onto the ground. By the time we got into the theatre, we were both soaking and the flowers were a bit battered looking. Kim was agitated, wondering where we were, as the show was about to start. When she asked us why we were so late, neither

Emma nor I were in the mood to explain. We were both stressed out and it took us a while to relax and get on with enjoying the show, especially with me having to sit in wet trousers and pants. Erin danced amazingly and deserved her bunch of roses at the end of the show, even if they were a bit battered looking.

Attending the show highlighted positive and negative issues for me. On the positive side, I got there, even managing to cope with a few challenges; facing my fears of being seen in public, coping with the rain and walking in the dark. On the negative side, it highlighted how much more difficult and time consuming it now was for me and whoever was taking me to an event. I now recognised that taking me out needed to be planned, to allow plenty of time to get me there, to avoid it becoming stressful. I couldn't be rushed, no matter how hard I tried. It also highlighted how much more difficult it was for me to access outside when it was raining or visibility was poor. In such circumstances, I needed to concentrate even more when walking to the car, due to the uneven surface of my drive and having no flexibility in my ankles.

Another first was to go to Dunfermline on the bus, in my electric wheelchair, with a friend Dot. Going on the bus was a scary thought, as I knew all the passengers would be watching me. But I did it. I knew that challenging my fears was the only way to make the most of my life and do every day activities. Manoeuvring my electric wheelchair on and off the bus was daunting but was manageable and what a difference it made. I hated shopping whilst in my manual wheelchair as I depended on someone pushing me to what I wanted to go and look at. I felt I intruded on their shopping experience. To be honest, it was not a good experience for me, as I was so dependent on others that it made me feel useless. So I often refrained from going. Being in my electric wheelchair meant I could go wherever I wanted to go, look at whatever I wanted to look at and feel less of a burden.

I had a lovely time that day, treating myself to some new items of clothing. We also went for a coffee on arrival and lunch later on in the day, with me feeling more 'normal' and upbeat than I had been for ages. I was out on a day's shopping, an activity I had always enjoyed, and for the first time, felt more independent, which was good. There was also a good, easily accessible disabled toilet in the centre, which put my mind at rest.

Whilst at the shopping centre, I noticed the Mobility Shop, so went in to enquire about what support was available. I found out that I could hire an electric wheelchair and use it whilst in the shopping centre. Although I had my own chair with me that day, it meant I could hire one in the future, if I was brought to the shopping centre in a car. I have used the service on a few occasions since then. It's a service I feel is of so much value to disabled people when out shopping, giving them the ability to have choices, be more independent and not be so reliant on others.

At last, I received my Mobility Car and was now able to take my electric wheelchair with me when I went out. I could sit in my wheelchair in the car, but preferred to sit in the passenger seat and be like everyone else, so my wheelchair would be wheeled up the ramp, at the back of the vehicle.

The down side of the Mobility Car was it was only insured for Kim and Sean. I had been led to believe that I could add other names to the insurance, once I had the car, but this wasn't as easy as I'd thought it would be. It turned out that I had to request a change of driver on the insurance if I wanted anyone else to drive the car, stating the length of time required. This was not always satisfactory, as the insurance company was not open on a Sunday or public holidays. It therefore meant, if anyone else wanted to take me out in the car on these days, it had to be pre-planned and outings could not be spontaneous. Another condition was that all drivers had to be over twenty-five years of age, which meant Emma was not eligible.

A few months later, I was made aware that my car could be insured on an open policy, as I had a care plan and received support from carers. This meant any family member or friend, with a clean driving licence, could drive the car. It became so much easier for me; I could go out in it whenever I wanted to.

CHAPTER 19

Facing Christmas Without Limbs

December arrived, the month I had been dreading, for lots of reasons. I had always enjoyed Christmas, buying and wrapping presents, writing Christmas cards, decorating the Christmas Tree and buying the food needed for over the festive season. This year I had no interest in any of it. It would magnify just how much my life had changed. I had no enthusiasm to go shopping, and I knew I would feel claustrophobic with so many shoppers rushing around. I couldn't put my tree up and decorate it with the care and attention I had always taken. I couldn't wrap presents, as even putting a gift in a gift bag posed problems - the limited span of my right hand meant I could only grasp items of a certain width and weight, and opening a bag and putting the gift in, was no pleasure. Writing Christmas cards and putting them in envelopes was also hard work. I could write one or two cards efficiently now, but to do this on mass, was daunting. Then of course, there was my inability to prepare food, as I now relied on others to do this for me. I just wanted Christmas to go away.

For many years, my friends and I went away to a hotel for a weekend break, usually the first weekend in December. We recognised earlier in the year that I would not be able to access the hotel we usually went to, so we opted to go to a lodge equipped with disabled facilities. As there were ten of us going, two Lodges were needed and we managed to source them at a reasonable distance from my home, with the lodges being next door to each other.

As going to the Lodge would be the first time I had stayed away overnight anywhere, I was very apprehensive and anxious about stepping out of my comfort zone. But I knew I needed to soldier on and try to live as normal a life as I possibly could.

On the day we were to go to the lodges, I had an appointment at Ninewells, to get my new prosthetic right leg. Previously I wrote about my leg having to be recast, as it was squint. It was now ready to be fitted. So, on route to the Lodge, my friend Florence, took me to Ninewells in my mobility car for the appointment. My left prosthetic leg had skin put over it, making it look like a real leg, rather than a steel pole. To take prosthetic legs off, there is a release button on the outer side. As I had no left hand, releasing the left leg myself was impossible. I wanted to be able to take them off myself, so the release button on my left leg, was resituated on the inside of the leg, allowing me to release it with my half thumb. However, my new right leg couldn't have the skin applied until I had tried it out for a couple of weeks. My legs looked weird, with one like a pole and one like a leg, but even having one leg looking more normal, felt amazing and I could not wait for them both to have their skins on.

I would return after two weeks to get skin on my right leg too, but by that time I had found out that it didn't fit any better than my last one had and it was hard to put on. As it was so near Christmas, I knew it would be too late for my leg to be recast for a third time, so chose to put up with it, until after the festive season.

We were first to arrive at the Lodge and I relaxed right away as the Lodge was equipped with everything I needed. In fact, it was so much better than my own house. The living area was spacious, allowing me to get around in my electric wheelchair. It even had a breakfast bar which was wheelchair accessible. The height of my bed could be adjusted, so I was able to slide onto it from my wheelchair. It had a wet room, with a freeway chair, similar to the one I had at home, and for the first time since my discharge from hospital, I was able to have a shower and wash my own hair independently.

The weekend was a great success. Being away from my reality, with my friends, having meals around the large dining table, sipping wine and cocktails, playing board games, with lots of fun and laughter, was just what I needed. Being with my friends meant I could be me, as they saw me as the Marguerite I'd always been, not the Marguerite with all her limbs missing.

My time at the Lodge also reinforced why building my new home was so necessary. It would provide me with all the facilities I had whilst I was there. For the first time since leaving hospital, I had felt more independent. The wet room meant I could shower myself, getting some of my dignity back and that on its own was massive for me. My new home would have a wet room and the space I needed to live more independently. I couldn't wait to move there. I recognised even more now, that living without these facilities, was having a negative effect on my mental health.

The building of my new house was progressing well and Sean sent me pictures regularly, keeping me up to date on how it was looking. I really appreciated that, as I was unable to access the house in my wheelchair.

Whilst still in hospital, I had recognised I did not want to be at home for the festive period and the girls felt the same. We decided that going away on holiday over Christmas and New Year was a good idea. Somewhere hot was a necessity, as I had always enjoyed my holidays in the sun. However, a beach or pool holiday was now not appropriate. I couldn't go on sand with my wheelchair, couldn't go in the sea, or swim in a swimming pool and couldn't lie on a sun bed, as it was too low for me to get on and off. And I didn't want to be on show. We needed a holiday, where we would be kept busy, so we had no time to dwell on how different things had been last year at Christmas. We weren't running

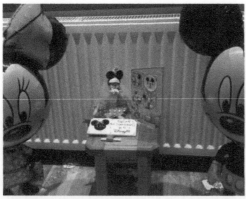

Figure 26; We're Going to Florida

away from reality, but we needed time away from it. We also needed to take Erin's and Gracie's needs into account as, although we wanted to forget Christmas, it was the most magical time of the year for them. So the decision was made that we would go to Florida, with Erin and Gracie finding out about the holiday on Erin's birthday in September.

*

A disabled villa was sourced, as was a car that would transport my electric wheelchair. Both items were necessities for me to be able to go on the holiday, but, as we discovered, as soon as the word disabled appeared on the requirements, the cost more than doubled in price. This just goes to show how disabled people are discriminated against and penalised. Why? It effects disabled people being able to afford go on holiday, and that is so wrong.

Our flights were booked for the 22nd of December, with us returning home on the 6th of January. Kim took on responsibility for all the preparations for our holiday. She thought of everything, from Minnie Mouse luggage with our names on them, personalised Minnie Mouse water bottles, Disney toilet bags, makeup bags, handbags and purses. She was determined it was going to be a holiday of a lifetime for us all.

I knew the holiday was going to be my biggest challenge yet, but looking back now, I think I pushed that to the back of my mind, choosing to focus on the need for me to be anywhere at Christmas, except at home. I disregarded the looks of shock I saw on people's faces when I told them where we were going, as I wasn't prepared to over-think it. I had learned from what I'd been through, not to over-think things, just take it one step at a time and focus on achieving success, accepting that the outcomes might not turn out to be what had been envisaged.

As the holiday approached, my anxiety did heighten, but I didn't show it. I remember lying in my bed, the night before our departure, thinking, 'What have I done? How am I going to manage?'

My friend Florence came around the evening before we were due to leave, to paint my toenails, as I'd be wearing my sandals. I'd been wearing socks and boots, since I'd received legs with skins on them, so hadn't seen my feet, but just assumed they would look the same as when I'd worn sandals to the wedding in August. How wrong was I? My feet looked alien, as I had no toes and this caused great hilarity, with even me, seeing the funny side. However, the dilemma then was, what I could wear on my feet, when in Florida? Fortunately, I was able to borrow Emma's trainers. They were not what I'd have chosen to wear on my

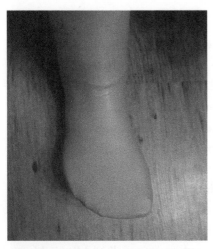

Figure 27; Where's my toes gone?

feet, as I'd never been one to wear trainers, but there were no other options. My boots were not suitable and neither were my leather slip on shoes. Both were winter footwear and I was going to the sun, where summer footwear was needed.

Kim, Erin and Gracie arrived on the morning of our departure to pick Emma and myself up at 5.50 am. Sean was not going with us, deciding to stay at home to continue to work on building my new home, during the holiday season.

Emma had done well, helping get me up and ready so early in the morning. So off we went to Edinburgh Airport. Erin and Gracie were wide awake and bubbling with excitement - not in the least bit tired, even though the had to get up so early when it was still dark outside.

Once at the airport, Kim parked in the disabled drop-off point and helped Emma take

Figure 28; Florida Here We Come

our luggage into the terminal, whilst I stayed with Gracie, unable to help. Only having my right hand to use to operate the controls on my electric wheelchair, I wasn't able to help with the cases. Kim then went to park the car in Airport Parking, before we headed to the check in desk. At the desk, I was asked if I had anything to declare and I informed them that I had an arm in my case, as I'd packed my prosthetic arm in my suitcase. I thought I'd better make them aware of it being there, as I didn't want it to show up on the x-ray machine and them think it was a real arm. I knew that the member of staff thought it amusing, but he didn't laugh until I made a joke about it. Once we were checked in, we headed to the Departure Lounge for a well-deserved breakfast.

The airport staff were very helpful. They led me in my wheelchair right up to the aeroplane door. I was first to get on the plane, along with my family and at the door, I had to stand up and walk onboard. It was scary, dealing with the slight slope and the different surfaces, as I had no pliability in my ankles. But with Emma's help, I managed it. I had recently bought a folding walking-stick and that helped enormously. I don't think I'd have managed to walk safely without it, even with Emma's help, as I felt more stable and secure, being able to balance with it. Once on the plane I walked nearly the whole length of the cabin, balancing myself by holding on to the tops of the chairs, as I made my way down the aisle. I had chosen a seat near the back of the plane, as it was nearer the toilet and it meant I only had a short distance to walk to it, when the plane was in motion. Once in my seat, the worry and anxiety I had felt about how I was going to manage onto the plane, began to disperse. I had done it!

On route to Florida, we stopped for a few hours at Newark Airport, New York, with the flight being around five and a half hours. Erin, fell asleep quickly, the early morning rise, having taken its toll and she slept for most of the flight, but Gracie was wide awake for the first stage of the journey. She was so excited at being on an aeroplane. Erin had closed the window blind and at one-point Gracie climbed over her and opened it to look out of the window. All she could see was blue sky and clouds and she turned around and shouted, "Granny, I'm flying!". She made us all laugh, and it made me realise, that even though I felt daunted by the two weeks stretching in front of me, everything was going to be alright. I would face lots of challenges ahead, but it was all going to be worth it, especially seeing Erin and Gracie embrace the Disney experience, particularly at Christmas.

I was frightened that my legs would get sore sitting on the plane for so long and they certainly were stiff by the end of the journey. But once I was up, I managed to walk off the plane, where my wheelchair was waiting for me. We had something to eat at Newark Airport and then it was back on another plane, arriving in Florida a few hours later, tired, but excited. Being disabled meant we were escorted through Customs and to the baggage hall. Then it was time to pick up our hired car. As it was late in the evening, the car was left ready for us to collect, but we had to wait on a mini bus to take us there. The long journey had taken its toll on Gracie and she proceeded to be sick all over her clothes, so she had to go on the bus wrapped in her Disney fleece. Kim did so well, puzzling out in the dark how my wheelchair was to be secured and driving on the other side of the road on route to the villa, with Emma using the Satnav to navigate. There were a few hiccups before we were able to enter the villa, but we made it, with having stopped at Walmark to buy breakfast for next morning too. It was very late when we arrived and we had been travelling for over twenty-four hours, so we went straight to bed, with Emma and I deciding to share a room.

I woke early in the morning, my stomach gurgling, and I knew I needed to get to the toilet as soon as possible. The problem was that I had no commode at the side of my bed and to go to the toilet, I needed to walk, so needed my prosthetic legs on. I woke Emma and asked her to put my legs on quickly, but putting my legs on takes time and them not fitting properly, meant it was even harder than usual to put them on. I had to stand up to get them to click into place securely. The bed was lower than my bed at home and a lot softer, so it was harder for me to sit on the edge. I felt as though I was slipping off it. Getting up from it was even harder and as I had to stand up to get my legs on, it was scary. I was frightened, I'd fall.

Emma was struggling to get my legs on and I was beginning to panic, so I asked her to quickly get a towel and a basin I could try to sit on, if I didn't manage to get my legs on in time to get to the toilet. She sat me on a towel, then ran to get Kim to help, with them both returning together. Emma came into the bedroom carrying a glass fruit bowel, saying that's all she could find. When Kim realised that Emma had brought it for me to use as a toilet, she became hysterical with laughter. Emma and I were laughing too, but I was laughing through panic and becoming increasingly distraught. I began to cry, as the situation only emphasised how disabled I was. I did manage to get my legs on and reach the toilet in time, but it took time for me to calm down. I slept with my legs on the next night, too scared it would happen again. After that, I think I became more accustomed to the villa and my surroundings, so felt safe enough to take my legs off when I went to bed. Looking back at what happened that first night of the holiday, it now seems funny and we have laughed many a time about it. But at the time, it was not at all funny, but very stressful.

Unfortunately, the shower cubicle in the villa was difficult for me to access, so we had to improvise. I kept my prosthetic legs on until I was sitting on a chair, just inside the cubicle. Once sitting down, the girls took off my legs and one of them held the shower head over me, whilst the other helped me wash. Meanwhile, I held onto the hand rail to keep myself safe. My stumps dangled out of the shower, so towels needed to be on the floor to avoid flooding the bathroom. Once showered, my stumps were dried and then my prosthetic legs put back on again, to allow me to pull myself up on my feet. As my legs weren't fitting well, this proved difficult at times and was very scary for me, as well being very undignified. The first time I did this, I was in tears. Kim and Emma were in tears as well at seeing me so distressed. But I knew if I didn't shower in this way, I'd have been unable to shower at all, so I had no choice.

The first morning of the holiday, I had lots of texts, as everyone at home were keen to know we had arrived safely and that everything was alright. My family had been phoning each other, asking if they'd heard from us, as they were beginning to think something was wrong. They were all relieved to know that we had arrived at the villa and that the reason we hadn't contacted them before now, was because it had been too late to do so, by the time we'd got there.

We had a lazy day at the villa on the first day of the holiday, with Kim, Emma and the girls, visiting Walmark for a Christmas tree, food and drinks. They returned with a plant in a pot (the nearest thing they could get that looked a bit like a Christmas tree) decorations for the tree and a wreath to put on the door. The tree was decorated, presents were put under it and the wreath was put on the outside door. Christmas was now official.

Figure 29; Our Christmas Tree

Kim, Emma, Erin and Gracie, spent time in the swimming pool and the jacuzzi. I knew before we went on holiday, that I couldn't go in the pool, or lie on a sunbed, but it was still hard to take. I would have loved to have spent time with my granddaughters, playing in the water. But instead of thinking too much about not being able to, I focussed on how lucky I was to be in Florida with them, seeing them having fun.

The next day was Christmas Eve and although my electric wheelchair had been put on charge overnight, it hadn't charged. We thought maybe we hadn't put the plug in properly, so we tried again. But it still hadn't worked and we realised the voltage was different in the USA, from when in Britain. We needed to source a charger, with the correct voltage. Kim went on-line and sourced a wheelchair rental shop nearby and on contacting them, they confirmed we could rent an adapter. So we set off there, to hire a charger, before heading to the first theme park of our holiday, Sea World. Although my wheelchair hadn't charged, there was still a good deal of charge in it as it had only been used at the airports.

We had a fantastic day. All the disabled facilities I needed were there for me, enabling me to relax. The Christmas decorations in the park, along with the Christmas themed activities, made it extra special and got us all in the Christmas spirit. We left the park around tea time and just before we reached the car, the charge on my wheelchair ran out. Emma had to push it the last few metres. On the way home, we picked up a Chinese take-away, planning to relax with a Christmas eve drink after our meal. But we were all exhausted and headed off to bed straight after we'd eaten.

Christmas Day arrived and I awoke with mixed emotions. Even though we had come on holiday, so as not to be reminded of how different Christmas now would be, I couldn't help dwelling on it. It felt strange being away from home and my family, at a time of year, when I was so used to being around them all. But I knew we'd made the right decision to be there in Florida, and Erin and Gracie coming into my room to wish me a Merry Christmas confirmed that.

We had our traditional croissants and 'Bucks Fizz' for Christmas breakfast, after opening the presents we'd brought with us from home. The girls received lots of cards with dollars in them, so they were excited at the prospect of spending it at the parks. They excitedly phoned home to speak to their dad, telling him what Santa had brought them. The girls would Facetime and phone their dad regularly every day during the holiday, updating him on what they'd been up too.

Having the correct charger for my electric wheelchair meant it was now fully charged and we could set off to Disney Springs, where Erin and Gracie were transformed into Disney Princesses at The Bibbidi Bobbidi Boutique, before we headed off to The Magic Kingdom, to spend Christmas Day there.

When entering any of the Disney parks, your finger print is taken as identification and as I had no fingers, Emma's finger print was given in place of my mine. Our first stop was the Information Desk, where due to being disabled, I was given a pass card that enabled me to book all the rides without having to queue. Kim was given a tag for Gracie's buggy, allowing her to take the buggy to the rides and not have to leave it in a buggy park. This meant she could help me, knowing Gracie was safe.

Having the pass card turned out to be so useful, as I didn't need to wait in large queues, with everyone towering above me. If I couldn't go on the rides, I sat beside Gracie in her buggy, while Kim, Emma and Erin had fun on the rides, knowing we were nearby. The Universal Parks used a similar system to the Disney Parks and it made visiting all the parks so much more accessible for me, diminishing many of my anxieties and making the experience so much more enjoyable for us all.

Christmas Day at The Magic Kingdom was amazing, with the Christmas Parade being truly magical. To see the expressions on Erin's and Gracie's faces, made the experience even more enjoyable. Christmas Day dinner, was a hot dog roll and curly fries, sitting on a wall, in the sun. So different to what our Christmas dinner at home would have been. There were a hundred thousand people in the park that day, so it was really busy. It was hard to believe so many people chose to spend Christmas Day at a theme park and that we were also doing just that. I kept having to remind myself it was Christmas Day, as it was so surreal.

We headed home, at the end of a busy, but fantastic day, creating lots of memories with the girls. Kim, Emma and I intended to sit and relax with a Christmas drink on our return to the villa, but yet again we were all too tired and so headed straight to bed.

We had a brilliant two weeks in the sun, in Florida, going to all the theme parks. We had been to Florida twice before and yes; it was massively different for me this time. There were many rides that I couldn't go on, but I'd known that would be the case before I'd gone, so I was able to accept it. I did not dwell on the negative points of the holiday, but focussed on all the positives, of which there were so many.

We spent New Year's Eve at Universal Studios, watching the fireworks display at midnight. Then we spent New Year's Day at EPCOT, visiting all the countries of the world. On another day, we visited Volcano Bay water park, and although I couldn't take part in any of the activities that day, it was

Figure 30; The Magic Kingdom at Christmas

great to see Erin and Gracie have so much fun on the water rides and play pools. Of course, we also had a day doing some retail therapy, finding many bargains.

Before we knew it, it was time to fly home. We stopped again in New York, but not without being delayed twice. So, we were all tired by the time we reached Edinburgh. It was cold and raining and for me, being home brought mixed emotions. It was nice to sleep in my own bed, but it also meant I was back to my new reality, which I hated.

Figure 31;
Happy Hogmanay from Universal Studios

CHAPTER 20

January 2019

Another year began and on my return from holiday, I was determined to start the new year with a positive frame of mind. I knew that going to Florida had been a huge challenge and I had achieved that. My family admitted to their concerns that I was taking on too much, flying all the way to Florida, never mind the challenges I'd have to tackle when I got there. It just emphasised how big an achievement the holiday had been. But I'd done it and it made me realise how far I had come, and how strong a person I was. I was determined to achieve even more successes.

My first priority on returning home, was to phone Ninewells and arrange an appointment to get my prosthetic legs fixed. The right leg had continued to be difficult to walk in. I walked awkwardly, with my foot bending outwards. I received an appointment for two weeks later and this led to my two legs being recast, as my stumps had shrunk yet again. Little did I know that I wouldn't receive my new legs until the end of April and that the next four months would be so difficult and stressful. Anyway, for now I would await another appointment, when my new legs were ready for fitting.

I fell for the first time in January. Because my legs did not fit properly, I had to stand up in them to get them to click into place securely. One morning when Emma was helping me get ready, I did this, but instead of them clicking into place, both legs gave way, detaching themselves from my stumps, and I fell to the floor with a thump. Once Emma and

I got over the shock, we laughed, but I think it was our way of stopping ourselves from panicking. How was I going to get up off the floor?'

Emma had the great idea of using my bath chair. As it was heavy to lift, she brought it through to my room on my freeway chair and put it on the floor next to me. I wriggled onto the seat and Emma then pressed the button to raise the chair from the ground. This enabled me to get into a sitting position and eventually try again with my prosthetic legs. Thank goodness they clicked into place this time. I have only fallen one more time since then and that was a few weeks later. Again, it was due to my ill-fitting legs causing me to lose my balance when trying to get up from sitting on my bed. Once again, the bath seat came to my rescue.

Moving to my new home meant I no longer needed to be given a bath. I was wheeled into the shower on my freeway chair. However, the bath seat went with me, as an aid to help get me up if I ever fell again. It also meant I could use it to have a bath in Kim's house, if I took the notion.

I was conscious that sitting so much meant I was more susceptible to putting on weight and I decided to go along to the local Slimming Club with my friend. As I was self-conscious of standing on the scales on my prosthetic legs, I arranged that I'd be weighed after most club members had gone. I went back the next week, having found dieting difficult as I wasn't in control of my own meals. I relied on meals my family and friends gave me, so a lot of the food I ate was not what the club recommended. I joked about taking off my prosthetic arm to make sure I'd lost weight, but I needn't have worried, as according to the scales, I had lost one stone, one and a half pounds. I knew that couldn't be right, but the club leader was adamant, and I was given my half stone and one stone achievement stickers. People congratulated me on my massive weight loss, saying, "That's amazing!" My response was, "That's a miracle!"

The next week, I went back to the club only to find out that I had put all the weight back on. I wasn't surprised, but I didn't return my stickers.

*

A friend requested that I do a talk about what had happened to me and my battle of recovery. Her seminar was 'Ignite the Fire', at the Rothes Halls, Glenrothes. I was apprehensive about doing it, not sure if I was ready to talk to an audience, especially looking as I did now. But I knew that if I could achieve this, it gave my life purpose and I so needed to have that.

Writing my story for the seminar was very emotional, as it felt like I was reliving what had happened to me all over again. I'd previously written notes on my I-pad, revisiting events during my illness so I could try and make sense of it all, and these notes helped me compile my speech. Condensing it into a thirty-minute talk, seemed to make it even more hard hitting. It was the first time I had spoken publicly about what had happened to me, and how I felt about it all. The feelings and emotions it triggered were hard to deal with. However, it also showed how far I'd come, and highlighted for me the strength, resilience and determination of the people who had helped me reach where I now was. I began to see that I did have an inner strength that had helped me cope and keep going. Of course, having a sense of humour was mentioned, as it had such a major part to play, throughout my journey and was part of who I am as a person.

When I practised delivering the speech for the first time, it was really difficult and I doubted my ability to remain in control at the seminar. Then I realised that if I cried, it wouldn't matter, as I was telling it from the heart and people would understand how emotional that would be for me.

By the day of the seminar, I had practised my speech several times, and I had cried on every occasion, But I felt ready to share my story and so was in a positive place by the time I arrived at the venue. My friend accompanied me, along with Emma. Kerry and her friend met us there, as Kerry had asked if she could be there too.

When sitting outside the room in my wheelchair, listening to my introduction, I felt panic begin to set in, but I took a deep breath, entered the room and faced my audience.

I never cried during the speech, but my voice did become shaky at intervals. I could see Emma and my friend becoming emotional at times, as for the first time, they were listening to my thoughts and feelings. They had been through the journey with me, but hadn't been aware of how it had really affected me and how I felt. It was hard for them to listen to.

I got a standing ovation at the end of my speech, with many of the audience in tears. I knew my story was hard hitting, as it highlighted how easily your life can change overnight. But it also highlighted how even when life throws you a massive blow, you can find the strength to fight back if you put your mind to it. The most important thing for me at this event though, was that it gave me the opportunity to highlight how serious contracting sepsis is, of the need to be aware of the symptoms and the importance of getting help as soon as possible.

Doing the speech really boosted my positivity and for the next two or three weeks I felt good. My new home was nearing completion inside and for the first time, I was able to get inside it to have a look for myself. I had spoken to my psychologist at times, about how I couldn't get excited about my new house, as I had no idea of how it was going to look. I had always enjoyed interior design and loved choosing colours and styles to make rooms come to life, but felt I now couldn't achieve that. I couldn't pop out to the shops to get ideas of what I would like, or even to purchase items, unless someone took me and that put me off going. I also couldn't make my own soft furnishings anymore and anyway, curtains were now not appropriate in my living-room, as they'd get in the way when going out of the French doors in my wheelchair. I couldn't pull them either, when opening and shutting them. While in the hospital, I left the curtains open during the night - I couldn't pull them shut or open.

After seeing my new home, I began to feel more excited about moving and could plan furnishing it with more enthusiasm. As I would be leaving all the furnishings in my old home, as Emma was to remain living there, I needed most things. I gathered the furniture I needed gradually, with a reclining chair and mobility bed already ordered, as two priorities. I had been sitting in my wheelchair daily since leaving hospital and the thought of being able to sit in a chair was something I was looking forward to.

I had recognised that having to use a wheelchair heightened the prospect of furniture being accidentally damaged, so good quality second hand items were purchased. I had never been a materialistic person, but was even less inclined to be that way now. Kim and I also visited Ikea to purchase all the everyday items I needed and were user friendly for my needs.

My friend had raised money for me by organising an Afternoon Tea Party, so she, another friend and myself, spent the day at the shops, buying soft furnishings. Friends and family had all been generous too, them buying me amazing items as house warming presents. I received all my kitchen white goods as gifts, as well as my television. How lucky was I to have such an amazing family and friends?

I became so aware of how much better my everyday life would be by living in my new home and I couldn't wait to move in.

*

I moved into my new home on Sunday the 3rd of February. Sean had worked hard to make that happen, recognising how much easier my life would be there. Although the house was far from being finished outside, inside was nearly complete, with only some small finishing touches still be done. As the driveway would be last to be done, a path of slabs was laid, allowing me to enter in my wheelchair, through the garage door and up a ramp into my new home. The garage door was operated by a fob, so I just needed to press a button to open and close it. In time Sean got CCTV cameras fitted and I was then able to see who was at the door when the doorbell rang, before opening it remotely.

I had Velux windows in my living room roof, which I could open and shut, again remotely and I could operate my heating through my phone. The blinds on my French doors were inside the glass, to help me avoid bashing into them, and the light switches were at a height I could reach from my wheelchair.

Both my living room and bedroom were spacious and the doorways and hallway were wide to accommodate my chair. The wet room was roomy, with the sink specifically raised to the height that suited me and the toilet was raised to the height of my wheelchair, so that I could slide off my chair onto it, if not wearing my legs. Every aspect of the house had been done to accommodate my needs and it looked amazing.

It took all day to move my stuff into my new home and the last items to be moved were my clothes. I became very emotional as I came out of the home, I'd lovingly renovated for the planned future I could no longer have. I knew my new home was where I needed to be, but it was another change and it made me feel scared and insecure. I was also leaving Emma behind to live on her own, and I felt so guilty. Her life had changed so much and she didn't deserve any of it. She'd had to cope with living on her own when I was in hospital and she was so happy when I returned home after six months. Now I was leaving her on her own again, but this time it was forever. There was a room at my new house if she wanted it, as a spare room had been built as part of the plans so that Emma or anyone caring for me could stay over, but she decided to stay in the home she was accustomed to. Emma could see I was crying and her emotions got the better of her too. We hugged each other, with no need for words. We both knew exactly how each other was feeling.

Kim and Emma took my clothes round in their cars, while I drove there in my electric wheelchair, as it was just around the corner. It was the first time I'd been on my own outdoors and it was scary, made even scarier as it was night time and dark outside. On arrival at my new abode, my new bed was still being assembled and I couldn't wait for it to be ready for me. I was tired. I think it was an emotional tiredness, as I couldn't take part in the move. I had to watch it taking place from my wheelchair and that was very frustrating and surreal for me. It was really hard to watch others do everything and not do it myself. Even my kitchen cupboards were organised by others, who made sure that everything was convenient. Top shelves were hopeless for me.

It was strange waking up in my new home the next morning, but I saw very quickly how much more independent I could become. Even before the carer arrived, I had wriggled out of bed and onto my electric wheelchair then gone into the wet room to go to the toilet, all on my own. So different from living in my old home, where I'd have to wait for help to slide onto my commode, with them then wheeling me into the bathroom. For the first time since having my legs amputated, I was able to go to the toilet during the night if I wanted to. I was no longer trapped in my bed after my prosthetic legs were taken off and to me, that was massive. I could now take my legs off during the day, if I wanted to, as I could get around in my wheelchair, being no longer trapped in my living room, as I had been for the last six months.

CHAPTER 20

February, One Year Later

February saw me feeling more positive about the future. Speaking at the seminar in January had been hard, but had highlighted how much I had achieved on my journey to recovery and had given me the opportunity to do something positive, whilst enabling me to feel more like me again. My working life had been all about helping others and I'd felt by telling my story, I'd been able to do that for the first time since becoming ill. I'd shown people by example, never to give up and to focus on the positives, rather than the negatives and it felt good. It boosted my confidence and I felt more positive about my own future.

Being in my new home had an immediate positive impact on my self-esteem. I no longer felt so trapped or that I was living in a prison cell and was no longer constantly reminded of the future I no longer would have. Having more independence felt good and being able to do so much more of my own personal care without support, gave me some of my dignity back and that felt so good too.

Anyone visiting me could see the positive impact my new home was having on me, on a daily basis. The ICAS carers, who were still coming every morning, would comment on how much more positive I was feeling, as did my psychologist.

Moving to my new home had been one of the goals I'd set myself and now I had achieved that, I needed to identify a new one. I'd recognised early on in my journey, that having goals helped keep me focussed and determined to succeed. I'd also learned to focus on one goal at a time, to prevent putting too much pressure on myself. To others, my goals might seem trivial, but to me, every goal I achieved was massive, as they all took so much effort, physically, emotionally or mentally. Focussing on the goals I set myself, also stopped me becoming too upset about how badly I was walking on my ill-fitting legs, whilst I waited for new ones to be made. In my new home, I could have stopped wearing the legs and used my wheelchair, but I didn't want to give in. I always used my trolley as support, which allowed me to have my mobile phone and door fob with me at all times. I knew if I fell, I could contact someone for help.

I was allocated a Social Worker. He visited me to complete a Support Assessment, which would allow a Care Plan to be compiled. This would enable me to take control of my own care package, by using Self Directed Care, which allowed me to employ my own personal assistants. Completing the assessment was very difficult, as I knew I had to be honest about how living without my arms and legs really was. It highlighted how disabled I was and how much help I needed with my personal care and food preparation in particular. It also reinforced, that if at times I was unable to wear my prosthetic legs, I was even more dependent on support. It highlighted how isolated I was, as unless someone supported me to go outdoors, I was stuck inside, only socialising with friends and family who visited. There were tears at times during the completion of the document, from both me and Kim, as although we both knew the reality of my situation, it was hard to admit how it really was. Reading the completed assessment was even harder, as seeing it written in black and white, seemed even more harrowing, with it being hard to comprehend that I was reading about myself.

The completed assessment in time led to me being awarded a package of care and I was therefore able to employ my own personal assistants. But that did not happen until the beginning of June.

The anniversary of me contracting sepsis was looming. On the 28th of February, it would be a year since I'd been admitted to hospital, very ill. I still struggled with not being able to remember the first week of my stay in hospital and when I looked back on the first few weeks thereafter, remembering how horrific it had been, I found it hard to understand how I had coped with it, as how could I have?

In discussion with my psychologist, I recognised I had to acknowledge the anniversary and mark the event in some way. I knew if I didn't keep busy, I would be depressed for the whole day, which wasn't a good thing. I needed to focus on feeling positive, well, as much as I possibly could.

I discussed it with Kim and Emma, family members and close friends. We decided that I should invite my family, friends and neighbours to celebrate me moving into my new home, whilst recognising the significance of the day and the fact that I had survived to be here, surrounded by the people that I loved, who had all played a part in my journey to recovery.

Life seemed to be getting back on track for me, when I noticed the stump that had been my middle finger on my right hand was tender and sore to touch. I was hoping it was hard skin, due to me constantly using it to text, but deep down I knew it was the bone, just below the skin. Before long, the stump looked inflamed, so a call to the Doctor's Surgery was made. A nurse paid me a home visit, but wasn't sure what it was. She acknowledged that my diagnosis was probably right, recognising that I had experienced it once before, whilst in hospital last May. I had required surgery then.

Kim contacted the plastic surgeon, who had done both operations on my hand and an appointment was made for me to meet with her. However, over the next few days, the bone began to protrude from my stump and it became more inflamed. One Wednesday evening, I was sitting at my friends dining table, when I noticed a red track-line coming from my stump and continuing half way up my lower arm. I had no recollection of how it had looked last time, but knew it was a symptom of Sepsis. Emma was sitting at the table and I asked her, if she could see the line and was it what I thought it was. Her face drained of colour and she nodded, saying we needed to contact NHS 24. My friend told me later, how impressed she had been with how Emma had dealt with the situation. She herself had begun to panic. Emma contacted NHS 24 and was told to get me straight to hospital, so Kim was called and the three of us set off to A & E Department, at Kirkcaldy Victoria Hospital. I was told by the doctor in Casualty, that ICU and HDU had been alerted that I was there. Hearing her say that, highlighted how serious the situation was, as up until that point, I hadn't been too concerned, as I didn't feel unwell.

I was informed that I was to be admitted into hospital and I would be given intravenous antibiotics. Kim contacted my brother to request he bring an overnight bag to the hospital for me. He and my sister-in-law arrived with my bag and I could see the concern on their faces. It was then that it hit me, of how scary this must be for them all. I couldn't remember the events they had witnessed on my admission to hospital last time, but me contracting sepsis again, must have made them all revisit the memories of what had happened and the emotions and feelings they'd experienced, seeing me so ill. They must have been panicking that they might be reliving them again and that must have been so hard for them to deal with.

I was admitted to Ward 33 and immediately given intravenous antibiotics. I was put into a four-bedded room and although I felt a little anxious at being in a room with others, knowing how people stared at my amputations, I coped with it better than I expected.

It was hard to get my head around being admitted to hospital, once again with sepsis. What made it even more surreal, was that it was a year to the month since I'd been admitted with it the first time around. Why was my body reacting in this way to infection? Was my immune system not working properly? Not even the consultant could tell me why and even until the present day, I don't have any answers to why it happened again. But it did and although at the time I coped with it well, the reality of what happened hit me hard. Would I now have to live with the fear that if I had any type of open wound, I could be susceptible to contracting sepsis again?

I was also very aware that I had caught it quickly, so treating it was straight forward. But, if I hadn't noticed it when I did and gone to bed that night, quite unaware, it would have been the next morning before medical help was sought. I was so aware that the outcome could have been so different. I was living proof of what can have happen if sepsis is not treated quickly enough. I was frightened when I thought about what could have happened on this second occasion.

The staff in ward 33 were all pleased to see me, even if under weird circumstances, and it was nice to have a catch up with them all. And of course, it wasn't long before the banter started again. We knew each other so well and they knew humour helped me cope, so it was used in abundance. 'V.I.P.' was written in felt tip pen on the white board above the headboard of my bed. I had been given a bunch of artificial marguerites and had stuck them on the frame of my bed, which made it resemble a memorial bench. Someone secretly wrote 'R I P.' on the white board, as I had joked that my flowers represented, 'Here lies Marguerite Henderson'. 'V.I.P.' did seem more appropriate though, as the staff did treat me like one. They made me feel special. Being in Ward 33 again, made me realise how much I missed them all and how special every one of them was.

As I should have been at physio on the Thursday, I phoned Kerry the next morning to update her and she couldn't believe I was back on the ward. She visited me later on that morning to make sure I was alright, showing yet again how supportive and caring she was.

I was in hospital for five days and as had happened the last time I was in hospital, meals were brought in by my visitors. One lunch time, my auntie and uncle arrived with a picnic. The difference this time was that I wasn't in my single room. However, staff were happy to provide us with cutlery and we sat eating a buffet of foods including, salad, coleslaw, cheeses, bread and crackers. When Kerry visited, she laughed at us sitting there, eating our picnic, saying it was like old times. She told my uncle that every time she saw him, he was eating.

I was attached to the intravenous drip for an hour every four hours and it soon became problematic. My veins had been through so much during the six months I was in hospital, that they kept rejecting the cannula, leading to my arm swelling up. A phlebotomist nurse, was called to reposition the cannula when this happened, even if it was during the night. By the time I was discharged, my arm and hand were covered in bruises.

My appointment with the plastic surgeon had been scheduled for the Monday morning, so it had been agreed with the consultant, that I would remain in Ward 33 until then and then be discharged and taken to my appointment at the Queen Margaret Hospital in Dunfermline, by Patient Transport. My brother was to meet me there. However, due to a breakdown in communication between staff, I missed my appointment.

It would be another two weeks before another appointment with the plastic surgeon could be arranged. The outcome was that an operation to cut the protruding bone was arranged for later on that week. In the interim, I was given oral antibiotics until I went back into hospital for my operation.

I knew that after the operation, my hand would be bandaged and that would cause problems with my ability to use my hand effectively. This raised concerns about how I would manage to eat or drink independently, but the bigger concern, was how I would manage to go to the toilet without help. I had discussed these concerns with the ICAS occupational therapist and as her office was in the hospital, she arranged to come and see me after my operation. We discussed what support I would need after my hand was assessed, and what restrictions my bandaged hand would cause me.

A few days later, Kim took me to The Queen Margaret Hospital for eight o'clock in the morning. Although I was to go to theatre and have a general anaesthetic, it was agreed that I would be able to return home later on that day. Being back in the ward where I'd been last May to have a similar operation, brought back so many bad memories. I was still recovering then, from the operations to amputate my limbs and I was weak and unable to do very much for myself. Nursing staff had to use a hoist to get me on the theatre trolley. I remember feeling vulnerable and frightened and exhausted.

This time, I was in a much better place and took the prospect of Operation Number 5 in my stride. The plastic surgeon came to see me to explain what she was going to do and approximately when I would be taken down to theatre. As she had operated on me twice before, she knew me and my family and enquired how we were all doing. This meant a lot to me, as it showed she was interested in us, recognising how all our lives had been affected by what had happened to me.

On the way to theatre that day, I met the ICU consultant who had looked after me and who had been one of the facilitators at the INSPIRE group I had attended. He inquired what I was doing going to theatre yet again and I explained why, stating that I intended this operation to be my last one.

I woke up in the recovery room, feeling a bit sore and was given pain relief, before returning to my ward.

My hand was bandaged up like a boxing glove, but I managed to hold a piece of toast, as my half thumb was exposed. But to protect the bandage, I held the toast with a napkin. I also managed to drink a cup of coffee, as I could put my thumb through the handle. As my prosthetic legs were off, I was back to using a bed pan until it was deemed I was fit to walk, but I didn't let it faze me, as it was only in the short term that I would have to do that.

Being just out of theatre, my 'obs' were done. My temperature was raised and they couldn't get a reading of my blood pressure. They couldn't put the cuff on my right arm, due to my right hand having been operated on and my left arm was not giving a reading. Two nurses tried, but failed and a doctor was called, but he had no luck either. Eventually a third nurse tried and managed to get a reading, by putting the cuff around my upper right leg, only to find my blood pressure was high too. It was decided that my 'obs' were to be done, every two hours, but this was abandoned after my plastic surgeon visited me. I remember her asking the nursing staff what they were doing and them explaining, my 'obs' were too high. She told them not to stress me, then looked at me and said, "You don't need stressed, do you Marguerite?" My reply was, "I no longer get stressed, as I've learned not to". Her reply was, "I bet you have!" She knew what I'd been through over the last year and recognised why I coped in this way. She also knew my 'obs' were usually good and recognised they were high due to me not having had fluids or food since midnight the night before, in preparation for the operation. She was right, as my 'obs' went back to normal as the day progressed.

The reality of having my hand bandaged and the issues this might cause regarding my personal care, led to the decision to keep me in overnight, to see how I managed. I wasn't surprised by this. In fact, I myself felt more comfortable at having time to adapt to the restrictions my bandaged hand would cause me. I contacted the ICAS occupational therapist (OT) and made her aware I was being kept overnight and she arranged to visit me in the morning, to discuss the care package I would need on my return home.

Kim, Emma and my granddaughters came to visit me and brought something in for me to eat, with us all sitting around my bed, eating our meal together. It was now so natural for my family to visit me in hospital and eat with me in this way, as they had spent so much time over the last year, in hospital with me. Gracie called the Victoria Hospital in Kirkcaldy, 'Granny's hospital' as she associated it with me being there for so long. She had been sixteen months old when I was admitted to hospital, so wouldn't remember a time when it wasn't part of my life.

I had no after-effects from the general anaesthetic and as I was prescribed pain killers, I felt no pain from my hand and subsequently slept well. After breakfast next morning, a staff nurse came to reband-age my hand. I'd spoken to the plastic surgeon the day before, about my hand being bandaged like a boxing glove, causing me difficulties, particularly when going to the toilet. So the nurse was asked to reduce the bandage, to a dressing, which was so much better. I was able to use my walking stick easily, even though my hand was a bit tender. After talking with staff about how I would manage to go to the toilet, we came up with the idea of me wearing a rubber glove on my right hand, with the fingers pulled up inside, and it worked. This meant I did not need help to go to the toilet, so when the OT visited me later that morning, I was able to tell her I would not need my present care package changed. I was so happy about that. Having to have a carer help me when I went to the toilet, would have taken away my dignity, which I'd fought so hard to get back when in Ward 33. The thought of that possibly happening, had been a source of worry to me, as I didn't want to go there again.

I was discharged from hospital with Co-codamol and Paracetamol for pain relief and a box of plastic gloves. I returned a week later to the Out Patient Clinic to get the stitches out of my wound, with my hand being assessed as healing well. The plastic surgeon inquired if I needed more medication for pain relief and I informed her that I'd not needed to take the medication I had received the week before. She was amazed I'd had no pain as I'd had my bone cut. I should have had pain! It highlighted that I had a high pain threshold, probably as a result of my body having to cope with the severe pain when I'd had my arms removed, and wasn't given the appropriate amount of pain relief by the anaesthetist.

My hand healed well and I learned to change my dressing on my own, which was sometimes needed to be done twice a day. Due to the fear of me getting it infected, I needed to keep the dressing on until the wound was totally healed. I couldn't wait to be dressing free, so I could stop wearing the rubber gloves when I went to the toilet. That day eventually came and I am delighted to say that I have had no other issues with bones growing through my stumps since.

I returned to Ninewells to be fitted with my new prosthetic legs and with the ongoing issues with my walking ability, I couldn't wait to get them. My left leg fitted snuggly, but the shape of my right leg left me in disbelief. It was a peculiar shape and even more squint than the leg I was wearing. I tried it on, but felt unstable when standing and therefore I found it difficult to walk. I couldn't understand why I was being given a leg that was so squint, as I knew, having worn a squint leg for months, the damage it had caused to my stump, with it now looking squint also. I knew that if I had to wear this new leg, which usually meant wearing it for around thirteen hours a day, my stump would become even more deformed. I refused to accept it and requested that a straighter leg be made for me instead.

I left Ninewells that day deflated, disappointed and in tears. I'd been so looking forward to having my new legs. I thought I was going to be able to walk better but was leaving the hospital no further forward. I'd hoped to get back to doing more productive work in the gym, as that had been put on hold since last September. It had been unsafe to learn new skills, such as walking up and down slopes, or walking outside on uneven ground and for now, my hopes had been dashed and I felt so frustrated.

At that appointment, I was also given a glove shaped hand to wear on my right hand. It had a knife attached, so I could use it to spread or cut. I did try using it when I first got it, but found that, due to the strength getting better in my own hand, making it more functional, I managed better without it.

The month of February had had been a challenging month for me, but I was determined to remain positive. I woke up on the morning of the 28th of February, a year to the day, from when I'd been admitted to hospital with sepsis, with mixed emotions. I still found it hard to see the events of the last year as reality and that it had all happened to me.

My living room had banners on the wall saying, 'Marguerite's New Pad.' Food and drink had been bought and the Champagne was chilling in the fridge, to toast the occasion. Preparations got underway, with my close friends helping prepare food for the family, friends and neighbours who were due to visit me.

Visitors started to arrive around 11 am and the last visitors left after midnight, testament to it being a great success. Many of the people who visited that day, had never been in my new home, so it gave them the opportunity to see round it. They all remarked how much living there would improve my life. Kerry, my physio, popped in on her way home from work, to help me celebrate and I so appreciated her being there that day. Of all the people who came along, she was the person who knew more than anyone else, how difficult the last year had been for me. She knew the amount of strength, emotionally and physically, that I'd had to acquire, to enable me to cope and achieve. I myself know I couldn't have done it without her commitment and dedication. She now felt like part of my family and her visit that day seemed natural, especially as she already had a relationship with many of the other guests.

My big sister had given me a 'Guest Book', for all my visitors to write in, but frustratingly, I forgot to put the book out, so this was done later. The comments, nevertheless, from everyone who took the time to write in it, were very appreciated and a memento I'll treasure for ever.

CHAPTER 22

The Anniversaries Loom

The next few weeks were difficult because of the ongoing problems with my ill-fitting right prosthetic leg. My brother attended my next appointment with me and I was given the squint leg, yet again, to try on. Then I was given a straighter leg to try. It felt so much more comfortable and gave me more confidence. But the prosthetist seemed to be determined that I would be better off with the squint leg, even after I raised the concerns again, that I had raised at my last appointment. I also stated that wearing two drastically different shaped legs would draw more attention to me and I knew I couldn't cope with that, as it was hard enough for me at present, to cope with the stares from the public. My odd-shaped legs would draw even more attention to me. My prosthetist stated that I couldn't focus on how they looked, as their cosmetic appearance was not the most important thing. But for me, it mattered. I needed to look as 'normal' as I could be.

A second opinion from another prosthetist was requested, to observe me walking on both legs, but before I'd been given the opportunity to walk on the straighter one, the one I preferred, it cracked and yet again I left Ninewells without new legs. I was beginning to feel my ability to remain strong was dwindling and that worried me. I knew I needed to remain strong to keep going.

The next day, I attended the first ever meeting in the Victoria Hospital of 'Finding Your Feet', a support group for amputees. There are 'Finding Your Feet' groups in other regions of Scotland, set up by Corrine

Hutton, the quadruple amputee. Corrine had visited me in hospital in May 2018. I didn't feel like attending that day, due to the events of the day before and how low I was feeling, but Kim and I went along anyway, with me trying my best to put a brave face on it.

I have continued to attend the monthly group meetings, with the group expanding in members every session. However, I am still the only quadruple amputee who attends and I know that will probably always be the case, as what happened to me is not normal. Activity sessions are organised for members of the group to participate in, but my lack of arms stops me taking part. I know they would try to accommodate me, by making adaptations, but that just makes me stand out even more from everyone else and I don't want to be like that. Maybe in the future, I'll be able to rise above how I feel now, as I know it puts barriers up for me. But not yet.

My psychologist could see the effects the saga of my legs was having on me and encouraged me to address it with my prosthetist at the next appointment. So, at my next visit to Ninewells, I was determined to be proactive and address the ongoing issue with my legs, once and for all. The straight leg wasn't there for me to try on, just the squint one and I ended up breaking down in tears, stating that I couldn't go through this anymore and that I felt like giving up on walking. My prosthetists spoke about me having been through so much over the last few weeks, but I knew I was upset due to the frustration with my legs. I therefore made him aware of this, stating yet again, how hard it was for me to walk at present, on the legs I had and the need for straighter legs to be made to help straighten my right leg. I also emphasised how much of an impact the present situation was having on my mental health. He agreed to have a physio look at me walking and that assessment highlighted weakness in my muscle and core strength. In my opinion this was caused through walking wrongly since the previous September, when the issue with my leg begun.

I agreed to attend physio sessions at Ninewells for two weeks, to work on my muscle and core strength. I was struggling to remain positive and when speaking to the physio at Ninewells, I became upset and made her aware of how frustrated and deflated I was feeling, and why. Having never known anyone with a prosthetic leg, the situation I found myself in was alien to me and so I had put my trust in the professionals who were supporting me, only to feel let down and not knowing who to trust. It was therefore arranged for the senior prosthetist to be present at my next appointment, which took place a couple of weeks later. At that appointment, my squint right leg was nowhere to be seen and a straighter leg was in its place. However, due to having been walking for so long in ill-fitting legs, I had developed bad habits, so I agreed to continue to attend two sessions of physio per week at Ninewells, to improve my walking in the new legs, before I was given them home.

I'd also been given another false arm, but this one had metal prongs on the end of it, instead of a hand. To make the prongs operate, I had to put a harness over both my shoulders and move them back and forward to make the prongs open and shut. This meant I could hold items with it, which would help if I needed to make things stable, to enable me to use my right hand to do tasks, like cutting, spreading, etc. However, its drawback was, that if I adjusted my shoulders, it weakened its ability to remain grasping an object, therefore letting it fall.

I agreed to bring that arm, and my glove with the knife in it, to the physio sessions at Ninewells and meet with the OT, to practise using them in a kitchen environment. Along with my prosthetic arm, this meant I had three arms in a carrier bag, when I travelled to Ninewells

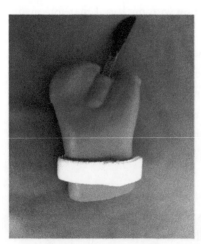

by Patient Transport. By the second week of physio, the crew driving me to my appointments, would call my bag of hands, my 'Handsbag.'

Whilst attending Ninewells for the two weeks, my left arm was recast. My prosthetic arm was now too big for me, as the swelling of my stump had reduced again. I would not receive my new arm until August, which was four months later, but the

Figure 32; My Glove Hand

174

summer months meant short sleeves, so there was no point in wearing a false arm anyway, as people could see it was false, so what was the point? My new arm would also have a different type of skin covering, to see if it would remain cleaner. I'd had problems with my arm becoming very dirty looking. It was uncleanable, making me self-conscious of how dirty it looked when I was wearing it.

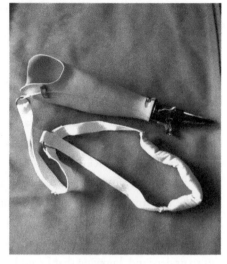

Figure 33; My Pincer Arm

I was given an elbow crutch, which fitted around my right arm to support me while walking and wearing my new legs at the physio sessions. For the first time I was able to practise walking up and down a ramp. As my ankles were not moveable, I had to balance myself using my knees and upper legs to enable me to stand up straight and not topple forwards or backwards, depending if I was going down or up the ramp, using my crutch to stabilise myself. This was really scary and I knew it was going to take a lot of practice, before I would feel safe and confident at doing this independently.

I also walked outside on grass for the first time and that also required me to concentrate on adjusting how I balanced. It was not a solid or flat surface, so my feet did not feel secure, again due to the lack of movement in the ankles.

At my last session of physio, I was given my new prosthetic legs to wear to go home. My old legs were put in a bag to take home as spare ones. I had no intention of ever wearing them again, as even looking at them made me feel upset, due to months of problems I had experienced. I left Ninewells that day, carrying two prosthetic legs and a bag with three prosthetic hands in it and thought what a surreal sight, I must appear to people who saw me. As for how I felt myself, I felt, I was living in a world that I didn't understand and that couldn't possibly be reality. How could it be?

*

The month of April was a very difficult month for me emotionally. The last few weeks had seen me cope with so many challenges and along with the ongoing saga with my legs, saw me reach breaking point. I was struggling to remain strong and see any positives. To be honest, I didn't feel like even trying to acknowledge there were any.

The first anniversary of my arms being amputated and then ten days later, the first anniversary of my legs being amputated, were extremely hard to cope with. I still found it hard to believe that the events of these dates really happened. I know that must sound hard for people reading this to understand, knowing that I could clearly see my amputated limbs and lived with the aftermath of what had happened, on a daily basis. But I really can't explain why I felt the way I did. It was how I felt though and it was all so overwhelming.

I couldn't help looking back at the month of April the year before, and wondering how I had coped with the horror I experienced. I recognised more than ever how my brain must have protected me from seeing it as it really was. It must have. How else could I have gone to theatre on the two occasions, as calm as I did. I should have been screaming from the top of my voice, "Please don't do this to me!" and I didn't. Flash backs of me lying in my bed watching my limbs die and then seeing them in bandages, often led to me struggling to cope; they confirmed the stark reality of the outcome of these events - the loss of my limbs and all that represented.

My birthday was to take place in April and I couldn't help but remember how I'd spent my birthday the year before - how I couldn't open my presents or cards on my own, how emotional the day had been.

Last year, I was on medication and going through the motions, taking everything as it happened. However, this year, I was on no medication and very much aware of everything and it was harder for me to cope with that. The reality was, I didn't want to celebrate another birthday, or think about the future. What did I have to celebrate? Another year living without my arms and legs! Why would I want to celebrate that?

The Friday before my birthday, my friends were around having a glass of wine with me as usual and asked if I'd like to go out for a meal to celebrate my special day. But I knew I wasn't in the right place to do that. I just wanted to forget it was happening. As they were trying to cheer me up, the doorbell went and Kim came into my living room carrying a box. It had been delivered from my work and contained all my personal belongings from my desk. I couldn't believe it! I hadn't been told it was being delivered and looking at my working career in the contents of the box, was too much for me to cope with. I was struggling as it was, trying to remain strong and not focus on the life I'd lost, but instead, focus on building a new, but different future for myself. I was trying so hard not to dwell on the past and here it was, staring me in the face. The box reignited the reality that I was no longer able to do the job I'd loved. It also brought back all the memories of my retirement not being acknowledged and having nothing to acknowledge that my working life had been meaningful.

As my friends were there, I held back the tears and asked my friend to bring me a black bag. I emptied the contents of the box into the bin-bag - all my certificates, my framed twenty-five years' service certificate, and personal items I had gathered during my working life. Why would I keep any of it? I would never use it again and I didn't want to be reminded of what I'd lost, or how horrible the ending of my working life had been. That night in my bed, I cried myself to sleep. Over the next week, I found it hard not to let my grief engulf me.

My birthday came and went quietly, with me fighting to keep myself from giving in and being defeated. My siblings took me out for dinner the weekend of my birthday and although I was feeling low, I did, as I always did and still do - I put my smiley face on to the world. I enjoyed spending the evening with my family, recognising how lucky I was to be surrounded by people who loved me and who wanted to celebrate with me. I'm sure, like me, they would have had their own thoughts that day, of how ill I'd been on my birthday the year before and thinking how lucky we were, to all be sitting there that evening, chatting over dinner.

I was also treated to a meal by my auntie and uncle, along with Kim and Sean, as Emma was working. I walked into the restaurant and sat in a normal chair. It was the first time, I'd left my wheelchair at home and that was something to celebrate, but at the time, I found it too difficult to see what an achievement it was.

CHAPTER 23

The Fight Back Begins

As the month of May began, the temptation to remain in bed every morning, not wanting to face another day, would have been so easy to give into. But I couldn't go there, as I knew if I did, I would find it hard to get up ever again. Talking to Lynne on a weekly basis at the hospital and meeting regularly with my psychologist, gave me the opportunity to talk openly about how I was really feeling and with their help, I was able to take each day at a time. During my journey, I had always concentrated on setting myself, one goal at a time, but I'd stopped doing that during the last couple of months, due to having so much to deal with, regarding my health and mobility issues. I now felt that my life had no purpose and I knew I needed to feel my life was worthwhile and that I had something to give back. But before I could do that, I knew I needed to get my positive attitude back and not dwell on how negative the last few months had been. I had to start by concentrating on regaining confidence, when walking in my new legs, I'd received at the end of April, which were now fitting me well, giving me the ability to work with Kerry, practising all the things we'd planned I'd be doing, when I'd left hospital and then couldn't, because my legs did not fit.

So, the fight back began. I returned to my physio sessions with Kerry and my walking improved. I got back to practising going up and down stairs and went outside to walk up and down the ramp at the A & E Department at the hospital. which was a few meters long. It was very daunting for me and practising doing it at such a busy place, where lots of people could see me, made me nervous. I knew it was killing two birds with one stone. I was practising the skill of walking on a slope, whilst letting the public see me. I was out of my comfort zone and I needed to get better at facing that. But, I did it and I felt so proud of myself, building on my ability to face my fears head on, which I'd felt I'd stopped being able to do, as my confidence had dwindled so much in recent months.

I went with my twin brother Jim and sister- in-law Brenda to visit my sister Dianne and brother-in-law Trevor in Ayrshire for the first time since becoming ill, taking my folding wheelchair with me, as I knew I still wasn't confident enough to walk into their house. We had a lovely day and had our tea in Nardini's in Largs, before setting off on the journey home. Before leaving the restaurant, I was wheeled to the Ladies, with me having to remove my prosthetic arm, to enable me to go to the toilet. When I came out, the sight that met me, was surreal, as there was Trevor, chatting away to my brother, whilst casually holding my arm over his shoulder. It did look amusing, but it also made me wonder, what kind of world I was now living in, when this scenario, was now normal for me to see.

After doing my speech in January, from which I had received tremendous feedback, I recognised that people were interested in hearing my story. Writing down what had happened to me had been good for my emotional well-being, just as my psychologist had predicted. It gave me the opportunity to revisit the events of the year before and see that although my ability was indeed limited, I had achieved many accomplishments throughout my journey to recovery. Now I realised I should use my records and tell my story. I decided to write this book. The reasons for writing my book are three-fold - to respond to the interest my story has created, to help raise awareness of sepsis, in the hope of alerting others that even with the smallest of cuts, speed of diagnosis is essential , and to shine a light for others who become seriously ill and have to go through a devastating life-changing experience, as I did.

I started writing my novel on my I-Pad, but was gifted a new laptop by my twin brother, sister-in-law and others, which made writing the book easier. It provided a more appropriate method for writing a large document and also allowed me to insert pictures, which evidenced different topics and made my story more realistic. As I had no fingers, I typed using my half thumb on my right hand, but as it became sore after typing for a while, I could only type for short periods of time. If I needed to add certain symbols in my text which required more than one hand, I'd push the appropriate key, using a stylus which I'd hold in my mouth. The Sun newspaper published a few articles about me during my journey and contacted me to inquire how I was doing. When I informed them that I was writing a book and they found out I was using my half thumb on the keyboard, they published an article about my achievement.

Writing my book was very difficult at times and often caused me to become very upset. I was writing about events that were difficult to revisit and which triggered emotions and feelings I had probably tried to keep locked away. But by writing them down, I was able for the first time, to relay the thoughts and feelings, that I'd felt during my journey and that was really helpful. I was

Figure 34; Writing my Book

aware however, that by doing this, the book could at times, make me seem full of negativity. But I had to be honest and show my story as it really had been to live through. If not, it would not have been a true reflection of how it really was for me.

I know that when my friends and family read this, they will find it upsetting. Although they were there supporting me from the start, I've never really divulged to them how hard it was and how I struggled to cope at times, particularly during the early days. I'd always portrayed a strong and humorous attitude to everyone and not let them see how I was really feeling underneath my positive exterior. I needed to be like that to remain strong, as my strength would have crumbled if I'd been given sympathy. I couldn't cope with that. I've never been good at receiving sympathy and would find it hard to have people feeling sorry for me, even more so now.

I sometimes feel like a fraud, for not being honest about how I'm really feeling and I've spoken about this often with Lynne and my psychologist. But it's how I manage to cope and it is part of my personality and how I protect myself. But more so, it is how I protect others, particularly my family and close friends. I never wanted them worrying about me. After all, I'm a survivor, always have been and always will be.

My friend June, who I've been friends with from our school days and lived nearby, was having a Cocktail Party at her house, during the month of May and I was invited. However, she lived in a two-story house, with the bathroom upstairs. This was a barrier for me attending. I had visited my brothers' and sister's houses and now managed to walk from the car and into their homes. I also now went for my tea to my friend's house nearby, on a weekly basis, climbing up four steps to be able to get inside. But in all these houses, their toilets were on the level and therefore accessible to me. To climb a flight of stairs to access the toilet was a much bigger conquest and one I felt unable to achieve. So the decision was made, that I'd go to the party, but that when I needed the toilet, I'd come home, leaving the party early.

At my next physio session with Kerry, I spoke to her about going to the party and my plan to come home, if I needed to go to the toilet. She was confident that I'd manage to climb the stairs and should not let that deter me. So, at that physio session, she took me to a flight of stairs in the hospital and I practised going up and down them, making me aware, that I was more than capable of doing it. But, my fear of climbing my friend's stairs was still worrying me. I would be climbing stairs which were carpeted, not on a smooth surface. I would need to be more conscious of lifting my feet higher when walking, to prevent tripping up. I also would be climbing the stairs in front of all the other guests attending the party and I hated being aware of people watching me. Walking up and down stairs needed so much effort, as I had to pull my heavy prosthetic legs up onto each step. Coming down stairs was even more challenging, as I needed to concentrate on supporting my body, as I took each step, to alleviate my knees giving way and me toppling over.

To do this in front of others seemed too difficult, again highlighting how hard I found other people seeing the challenges I faced. I hated drawing attention to myself.

So on the day of the Cocktail Party, my plan was still to return home if I needed to go to the toilet and the two friends who accompanied me to the party would come back to my house for a drink. However, after having enjoyed a few cocktails, I needed to go to the toilet, but didn't want to go home, as I was having such a good time. I could tell my friends were enjoying the party too, but being the good friends that they were, they didn't say anything, putting my needs before their own. So I made the decision to go for it and climb the stairs with the support of my two friends. One stood in front of me and the other behind me, to make me feel secure. I deliberately made myself forget about all the other people at the party and thoughts of them watching me. I focussed on the job in hand and it worked.

I walked up and down a full flight of stairs in my friend's house. This removed the barrier that had prevented me from visiting people. What an achievement! I felt so proud of myself, as I recognised, I had the strength and ability to keep fighting back and become more independent than I had ever thought possible. Looking back now, I think that night was when my confidence reignited. The last few months had seen it disappear and I'd found it difficult to begin to get it back. But it was returning, and from then on, it grew, as I achieved more and more fine and gross motor skills.

Shortly after attending the Cocktail Party, I was invited to my cousin's barbecue along with my siblings and cousins, and as he lived in Montrose, I knew I would have to stay overnight. The prospect of staying in a hotel room on my own was daunting, but I knew I had to continue to challenge my fears, so my twin brother Jim was tasked with finding a hotel which was suitable for my needs.

On arrival at the hotel, I discovered that my room, was in a different building to everyone else's. This heightened my anxiety right away! Then on entry to my room, I realised I could not access the shower or use the toilet without having my legs on. But the room was big enough for me to get around it in my wheelchair and I could transfer from my wheelchair to the bed, so it wasn't all bad. I recognised that there would be issues wherever I went. Even when in Florida, there had been problems with me utilising the bathroom and I'd coped, so I knew I'd be alright.

I enjoyed spending time with my family that weekend and even took part in a pub crawl, only declining going into the last pub we visited as it was too busy and everyone seemed to tower above me, when I was sitting in my wheelchair. Once back at the hotel, we had a nightcap in the bar, before heading to my room, with my family making sure I was okay, before leaving me on my own. I didn't sleep well, but that was normal for me and I coped with not being able to go to the toilet once my legs were off. I managed to get washed and dressed, before my sister Dianne and sister-in-law Brenda, came to put my legs on. Then we all met for breakfast, before heading home. I felt a great sense of achievement, knowing I had faced another challenge. I had stayed in a hotel room on my own, whilst facing my fears and not letting barriers stop me from succeeding.

At the beginning of June my Self-Directed Support began. This meant the end of the support I'd received from ICAS since leaving the hospital. Although I looked forward to having my own personal assistants, I did feel anxious about losing the carers with whom I had built up relationships. But, it meant I'd have the same assistants caring for me all the time, giving me consistency. Becoming an 'employer' was daunting, but after it was up and running, it soon became obvious how much more beneficial it was for my needs.

Also, at the start of June, for the first time since contracting sepsis, I used my sewing machine. I never thought I'd be able to use my sewing machine again, so it was a big milestone for me. Yes, I had learned to sew on a button, or mend a small hole in an article of clothing, but to use my machine took sewing to a different level.

Kim had been using my sewing machine and I decided to give it a try. The neck on one of my tops needed to be taken in, so I decided that I would try to fix it myself. I managed to fill the spool with the thread and then thread the needle, which is an intricate procedure and without my fingers, it was difficult for me to do. Then, with the use of my stump, I fed the material through the foot of the machine, keeping it in place, whilst I worked the peddle, using the foot on my prosthetic right leg. After completion, I did need help to trim the fabric, as even when using my disable friendly scissors, I was unable to cut the material myself. But to manage to alter a garment on my own was a massive achievement for me, even If I did need some help along the way.

Kim, Sean and the girls, went on holiday in June. It would be the first time I had been on my own in the house and it was a daunting thought. However, my personal assistants, family and friends visited me daily, making sure I was ok and to be honest, I coped better than I thought I would. Kim and Sean left their two dogs and they made me feel more secure as well as being good company. My friend and my next-door neighbour made sure the dogs were given a daily walk, a task I would have carried out in the past but could no longer do.

Figure 35; Using My Sewing Machine for the First Time

Sean had CCTV installed before going on holiday and I was able to see who was outside when the doorbell rang, before I used my remote control to open the door. I felt safe and secure at all times.

One day I went out with my friend in my mobility car. On arriving back at the house, as my friend was parking the car, a text message popped up on my phone from Sean, requesting that my friend park the car further down the road, as a skip was being delivered the next morning. Sean had the CCTV on his phone, but it was funny to think he could see what was happening at the house, when he was abroad on holiday. There have been a few funny incidents witnessed on the camera, all in good humour, but it is a really helpful piece of equipment, particularly for me when I'm in the house myself.

My Icerosses, which if you remember are the silicon gloves with the rivet on the end of each of them, which are placed over my stumps and attached to my prosthetic legs to keep them securely in place, were showing wear and tear. They no longer fitted snuggly to my stumps and were rubbing against my skin, causing irritation and redness, which could result in blisters. If this occurred, I knew I'd be unable to wear my legs, so another visit to Ninewells was needed, with new Icerosses being ordered.

My brother drove me to my appointment at Ninewells and on the way back home, we stopped to have a coffee. We parked on the road, along from the shop. That was the first time that I walked from the car and along a footpath. Once inside, I sat in an ordinary chair, like everyone else, with my wheelchair being left outside, in the boot of the car. It felt good to have entered the café, like everyone else, with me then sitting at the table, drinking my coffee and chatting with my brother. It was another of my goals that I'd now achieved and my next goal would be to walk from my home, to a car and from the car, into a restaurant. To achieve that I'd have to walk down a ramp, along a path with a gradient and then along the pavement, which was uneven. Then I'd also be similarly challenged, once I arrived at the venue. All of these outside surfaces were hard for me to walk on as my prosthetic legs had no flexibility in the ankles, so I had to concentrate on making sure I balanced effectively, to prevent falling.

The opportunity for me to achieve the above, happened a couple of weeks later, when I went out for lunch with my Auntie Nan and my cousin June. Walking down the ramp and being on different surfaces was scary, but I did it, with the aid of my arm crutch and the support of my cousin. They say, practice makes perfect and this is true, as my ability to walk outside and on different surfaces has gradually become easier. I do still need someone with me and think always will - I know that if I fall, I wouldn't be able to get back up. Their presence gives me the support I need, to keep me calm and focussed and keep my balance, to enable me to walk safely.

CHAPTER 24

The Summer of 2019

Unfortunately, due to issues out-with my control, the garden area of my new home was not finished for the summer, so I was unable to sit outside in the sun. That did affect my emotional well-being, as I felt trapped inside. Unless someone took me out, I was stuck in the house. I often felt like I had swapped my hospital room for my living-room and thought the world was going on outside my four walls, without me in it. It's not that I was on my own a lot, as I received lots of visitors and I really appreciated their support, but I needed to get out.

My friend Dot came down once a week and we went for a walk. Well, she walked and I sat in my electric wheelchair. We mostly went to Lochore Meadows Country Park as it was on my doorstep, often stopping at my mum and dad's remembrance bench which is situated in the park and would sit there for a short time, before heading to the café for a drink. I also went shopping or for something to eat, with my friends Mary and Raymond and really appreciated them taking me out.

I remember on one occasion, being out shopping with my friend Irene and a neighbour stopping me to say hello. They then asked me if my friend was my carer and I felt my stomach flip, as I thought, "Is this how people see me?" My friend, must have known what I was thinking and replied "Nah, I dinnae care about her!" making me laugh, before she told my neighbour that she was in fact, my friend. It was a typical Irene response. She was one of my closest friends and who I was now hadn't changed how we were with each other, always joking and seeing the funny side of things.

The holiday period meant that everyone was talking about holidays and it reinforced how I couldn't just decide to go away on a last-minute holiday deal like everyone else could. My holidays would now need to be planned, to make sure all my needs were met. I'd loved going on holiday, sunbathing, going to the beach, swimming in the sea or the pool, strolling along the promenade, spending time in the curio shops and markets, sitting sipping a drink in a café, people watching. Now, I was unable to do most of these activities and that was hard for me to deal with.

Over the summer, I again visited my sister Dianne in Ayrshire, with my older brother Willie and sister-in-law Linda. This time I walked into her house, which is an old cottage in the country. An area of the driveway was chipped, so walking to her door was challenging for me, but I did it with the aid of my arm crutch. Once inside, walking on carpet on old floor boards was another challenge, testing my balancing skills. I had a lovely day and before setting off for home, we all went for a meal at a local restaurant. I walked from the car park into the venue, which challenged my walking ability yet again. The walk was longer than I thought it would be and once inside the building, the walk to our table was nearly as long again. But I did it and it allowed me to sit on a chair at the table, like everyone else. Mind you, the walk back to the car was hard going. My legs become tired as the day goes on and because it was evening time, walking was more difficult. My brother parked the car nearer the restaurant door, to reduce the distance I had to walk, but I was still exhausted by the time I got into the car. But it was another achievement for me and meant that from then on, trips to eating places with family and friends, were planned at venues I could access by walking. No more sitting in my wheelchair at the table!

During July, Kim and Emma were dealt another blow, when their dad died unexpectedly, due to similar circumstances to myself. They had been through so much already and having to go through more heartache, was hard for me, as their mum to witness. I felt, I couldn't support them as I would have liked to and it was hard to watch them suffering. Their dad died at 54 years of age, the age I'd been when they thought they were to lose me. How could this happen to them again? Life was being so cruel to them. I am so proud of them both, as yet again, they showed an ability to cope, with strength and dignity beyond their years, and a resilience to adversity that was truly inspiring.

The next couple weeks were hard for all of us. We spent time talking about the memories we had of their dad, looking at old photos and playing his favourite songs. Kim, being his next of kin, helped plan his funeral along with his family and Emma, and I'm sure he would have been so proud of both his daughters. They both showed maturity beyond their years, having to say goodbye to their dad way too early.

Getting back on track, proved difficult. It had been a hard few weeks and had affected me emotionally, more than I'd realised. It seemed to trigger me again into analysing the events of when I'd contracted sepsis and this effected my ability to sleep even more than usual. As I've said previously, I hadn't slept well throughout my journey, but I now spent most of the night awake. It made me feel groggy and lacking in energy during the day. But I knew I couldn't give in, when I'd fought so hard up until now, so I focussed on continuing to build on my ability to walk confidently and add to the skills I had already mastered.

It wasn't until August that I got my new prosthetic arm, which had been recast in April. But I had grown in confidence in going without my arm in the months leading up to then and had developed a lovely tan. I wore sandals and painted my false toe nails, as that's what I'd have done before I'd lost my legs. Unfortunately, my sandals dyed my feet, making me unable to wear any other footwear, as the black dye was visible and I didn't need anything else to draw attention to myself. It did lead to lots of jokes being made about my black feet, by my friends, but the reality was, it was something else that I had to deal with.

Rockore 2019 took place on the 17th of August. It was hard to believe it was a year since I'd attended last year's event, the day after I'd been discharged from hospital. Looking back, I couldn't help but recognise how far I'd come since then. I had been able to do very little for myself and now I had acquired so many skills. I had become more independent and more mobile, and more confident in my ability to walk.

I had a great time at the festival with my friends. Even the rain didn't dampen our spirits and I stayed at the festival till the end. Arriving home, yet again had me thinking about how things had been for me the year before. I'd needed so much help from my friends back then, with them helping me get into bed and taking my prosthetic legs off. This year, I said good bye to them at the door. I got myself ready for bed and took my prosthetic legs off by myself. What a difference a year had made.

When I went back to Ninewells at the end of August, my legs were recast, so that I could be given a set of legs that I could wear when in the shower. This was to enable me to walk into the shower and wash myself whilst standing, instead of sitting in my freeway chair to shower, as I do at present. A referral was also to be made to WestMARC in Glasgow, where I would be fitted with legs with ankles that would move and adjust when walking on different surfaces. Ninewells could not provide me with those types of legs.

At WestMARC, I was also to receive my bionic arm. I had waited so long for this. My left arm was now deemed ready to have one fitted and I was to receive my first appointment in the near future. So, for now, all I had to do was wait for my appointment.

When I finally receive them, all three limbs will need to be plugged in and recharged overnight. It does make me think I'm going to be the nearest thing to looking like Frankenstein. All I need now is the bolts in my neck, but I can assure you that I don't intend to pursue that challenge.

CHAPTER 25

Still Trying to Find Me

Even though I knew how far I'd come, I still didn't feel a sense of achievement. My mood began to slump, but I didn't give in, to how low I was feeling and continued to work towards achieving more, hoping it would make me feel better.

My sleep pattern was worse than usual and I often ended up watching television during the night, in my bed. I had watched a programme which had a scene where a funeral took place and when I eventually fell asleep, I dreamed of my funeral taking place, with my coffin only being half the size it should have been, as I didn't need room for my legs. When I went to physio the next day, my friend who is also an amputee, was in the gym too. He said that I looked tired. When I told him I hadn't slept well, and related what I had dreamed about, he began to laugh, asking Kerry to come over, so I could tell her about my dream too. Between the laughter, she added to the hilarity by informing me that my coffin would be weighted down with sand bags, to stop it from tipping, due to my legs being missing. We did have a good laugh about how bizarre the situation was and it did cheer me up. However, the reality was, it wasn't really funny, as even with how ridiculous and comical it seemed, for me it was real.

*

Erin's dance crew had been awarded World Champions and were to appear in a show at the Carnegie Theatre in Dunfermline. I went along with Kim to see her perform. It was pouring with rain, so I decided to use my folding wheelchair to save walking, as I knew I'd be soaked, as I couldn't walk quickly enough. Getting me from the car to the theatre was challenging and once inside, I felt overwhelmed, sitting in my chair, with everyone towering above me. Kim wheeled me down to my seat in the theatre, situated at the end of an aisle. I couldn't stop feeling sorry for myself, as going to events, emphasised how much my life had changed. Someone along the row from us, said that the show we were about to see was very humbling and that once I had seen it I would never feel like moaning again, to which I replied "Yes I would." They then said that some of the children taking part had no shoes, to which I'd replied, "I have no feet." After I watched the show, I felt terrible, having been so selfish and moany. She had been right, a group of children from Africa were headlining the show and on hearing their plight, it did reinforce me realising the positives in my life and appreciate what I had.

A few weeks later, for Erin's birthday, I went with Kim, Emma, Erin and Gracie to see Mama Mia at the Playhouse Theatre in Edinburgh. I'd told Kim that I didn't want to sit in the disabled seats, as I knew they were at the back of the theatre and not a good location for the girls getting a good view of the stage. However, a week or so before we were due to go, I discovered our seats were in the stalls, which meant I had to go down forty stairs to get to it. Kim had thought the stalls were on the ground level, but they were in fact in the basement. On checking the Playhouse website, the seats that were available on the ground level, would not have been suitable for the girls, as their view wouldn't have been very good, so I made the decision to go down the stairs. When I told Kerry at my next physio appointment, what I was planning to do, she told me, I could do it and that if I managed it, then I would be able to do anything.

We arrived at the Playhouse early, with me in my electric wheelchair, hoping to avoid the crowds. But we had to wait, as the stairs to the stalls were closed to the public, so after parking my wheelchair in the bar area and going to the toilet, as I knew I wouldn't be able to go again until the show was finished, we went to wait in the queue. I could feel my anxiety rise, as I stood looking at the stairs, realising that at the top and bottom of each flight of stairs, there was a square pillar, which was a metre wide, with nothing for me to hold on to.

When we were allowed to descend the stairs, I focussed on each step, blocking out the people around me and began to go down, one step at a time, using my arm crutch for support and pressing against the pillar with my stump, until I got down far enough to use the handrail for support. I was terrified that I'd fall and I knew Kim and Emma could sense it, as they encouraged me to keep going, step by step, I couldn't hide my anxiety. Some people stopped and asked if they could help me, but I knew, that the only way, was by doing it by myself.

Finally, I made it to the bottom, only to find, that once in the auditorium, I had another few steps to go down, again with no hand rail for me to hold on to. Then with the girls encouraging me with every step I took, I walked down the aisle, which sloped downwards until eventually, I made it to my seat, which was near the stage, at the front of the theatre. By the time I sat down, tears were running down my cheeks and when I looked at Emma, she was crying too. I knew I needed to be strong for her and calmed myself down. This was meant to be a happy outing for us all, so I gave her a smile and focussed on enjoying the show. But I couldn't help thinking, as I watched people walking to their seats and sitting chatting, how, that when I'd been to the Playhouse previously, I had been like them. Able to sit in any seat I wanted, without all the barriers I faced now and I couldn't help but ask myself, "What has happened to me?"

At the end of the show, I waited until everyone left, then walked back up the aisle and started my climb, back up the four flights of stairs. After I'd climbed the second set of stairs, I could feel my strength dwindling. My prosthetic legs are heavy, with it taking a lot of strength to lift them up each step. Kim knew the effort it took to climb stairs with prosthetic legs and asked me if I wanted to sit down and rest. But I knew that if I stopped, I would find it difficult to get going again, so I kept climbing, feeling like I was climbing a mountain, with the summit, nowhere to be seen. By the time I reached the top, I had no energy left. Kim ran to get my wheelchair and I slumped into it, so glad to at last be sitting down.

The next morning, I could not get out of bed, as I was so tired. I didn't get up until midday. I knew what I had achieved the previous day, by walking up and down forty stairs, whilst in a busy theatre, was some accomplishment, but all I could think about, was how hard it had been and how frightened it had made me. I also knew, I would not be doing it again in a hurry, as even thinking about it, raised my anxiety levels.

That afternoon, I went out in the fresh air with my friend and it gave me a chance to blow the cobwebs away and put it into perspective. It was a massive achievement and although it had been hard to do, I had done it.

*

However, over the next few weeks, I found it hard to keep up beat. I think the experience at the Playhouse had highlighted how much my life had changed and how everyday tasks took so much effort and probably always would do. This again affected my ability to remain positive. My meetings with my psychologist and Lynne, gave me the opportunity to talk through how I felt and helped me keep fighting, determined not to give in to how I was feeling and I didn't.

My walking ability got better and better, with me walking within my home using no aids. By evening, my legs would be tired and I would have to use my walking aid, but I could cope with that. I was even more confident at walking outside, being less frightened of the possibility of falling, when walking on the uneven ground, as my ability to balance accordingly, seemed to becoming a normal reflex. But for safety reasons, I always had someone walk beside me.

I attended my twelve months follow up assessment with the INSPIRE group, at the beginning of October. I spoke about attending this group earlier in the book, explaining that it was for people who had experienced being in a coma. I'd attended a six-month assessment in March, but this one felt more poignant. Physically, I had improved drastically in six months. In March I'd been assessed as being able to walk ninety metres in six minutes using my arm crutch. Now I could walk one hundred and seventy meters in that time. The strength in my right hand had also improved drastically. In March, my strength had measured two kilograms, whereas now, it measured eleven kilograms, a drastic improvement. Through time, my hand had become stronger, and could hold heavier items. It also had much more flexibility and the improvement in

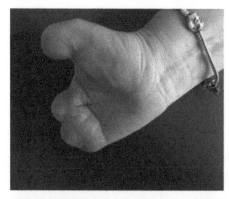

Figure 36; The Palm of my Right-Hand

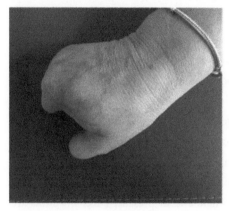

Figure 37; My Outer Right-Hand

my fine motor skills meant I could write more than a few words, even if the neatness of my writing was inconsistent. I don't think my signature every looks the same twice.

However, my emotional well-being wasn't so positive, with me talking openly about how hard it was to cope on a daily basis. Having to recognise that I would need help with my personal care for the rest of my life was still hard for me to accept. I needed help to go in the shower, put my legs on, put deodorant on, put some of my clothes on, put jewellery on, to name but a few tasks, I could go on and on. Then there were all the everyday things I couldn't do. I jokingly spoke about the time I'd been given a Chocolate Orange and couldn't grasp it in my hand, never mind open it, or break it into segments for eating. It was funny, but in reality, it wasn't, as it highlighted another task I could never achieve.

I've previously spoken about no longer feeling like me, as even the clothes I wear, are for practical reasons. The clothes, shoes and accessories, that did represent me, are no longer in my wardrobe. This is difficult to accept and continues to cause me anxiety and stress.

I began to come to terms with my inability to accept the life I now found myself living, and realised it was possibly due to having been in a coma for more than a week, at the start of my journey. I had been unable to acknowledge what had happened to me during that time. I felt that

I needed to know the details of those lost days, with the hope that I could then put the past to rest and move forward more positively. I had previously spoken to my psychologist about how I was feeling and she had encouraged me to talk to the ICU staff that attended my INSPIRE twelve-month assessment. The outcome of that, was it was agreed that a time would be made for me to meet with the ICU consultant and be told the details of my time in ICU. Because hearing the details of what had happened to me, might be hard for me to handle, it was decided that my psychologist should be in attendance as well. This meeting is still to be arranged, but I am hoping it will help me put the past to rest and move on.

The possibility of me becoming a volunteer at the group was also discussed. I had an idea what that entailed, as there had been volunteers present when I had attended the group last year. I'd previously spoken to my psychologist about it and I knew she'd already spoken to the INSPIRE staff about my involvement. I would have to wait until I received the training needed to be a volunteer in the hospital, but I am enthusiastic about the prospect. It will hopefully give my life a purpose again, as at present I feel I don't have one. There is also the possibility of it leading to me doing more voluntary work in the hospital. My working life had been about helping others and at present, I feel my skills are lying dormant. It will hopefully give me the opportunity to use them again.

After my twelve-month assessment, I was sitting chatting to Kerry and the INSPIRE staff, who I now knew so well, when another ICU consultant arrived. He'd bought a bag of apples at the fruit and vegetable stall in the foyer of the hospital and after saying hello to me, he asked if I'd like an apple. I couldn't help but look at the staff I'd just been talking with and had been telling them the story of my friend bring me a present of a chocolate orange, not recognising that I wouldn't be able to hold it, never mind open it, or break it into pieces. "Does Chocolate Orange ring a bell?" I asked. Everyone laughed, but it did emphasise how life was for me; a simple task like holding and eating an apple is unachievable.

It was around this time that a surreal situation took place. I was sitting in my living room, when the doorbell rang. My son-in-law answered the door and then came through to see me, with a smirk on his face. He had opened the door to be informed by the person standing on the doorstep, that she was a chiropodist. He informed her that she must be at the wrong address, as I had no feet. I would have loved to have seen the look on the poor chiropodist's face when he told her this. I had to admit it was funny.

After my meeting with INSPIRE, I couldn't stop dwelling on all the things I couldn't do. I knew most of them would never be manageable for me, but felt that getting myself in and out of the shower, preserving my dignity, would make me feel so much better and I so wanted to achieve this. One night after tossing and turning in my bed, thinking of how I could manage it, I had a plan. So, in the morning, I pushed my freeway chair out of my wet room, whilst in my electric wheelchair, placing it backwards against my bed. I then drove my wheelchair up against it, with the chairs facing each other. With the freeway chair now sandwiched securely between the bed and my wheelchair, I wriggled onto the freeway chair and once sitting securely, I moved my wheelchair out of the way, using the controls. I then jerked the freeway chair bit by bit, until I was back in my wet room. After managing to close the door, I jerked myself under the shower. After showering, I dried myself off and jerked myself back out of the wet room, manoeuvring myself back against my bed. I then used the controls on my wheelchair, to put it back up against my freeway chair, so that it was again sandwiched against the bed. I then wriggled back onto my wheelchair, then pushed the freeway chair back into my wet room, before going back to my bed in my wheelchair, where I then wriggled onto the bed. I'd done it! When my carer arrived to help me get dressed, I was sitting in my underwear, having dried and straightened my hair, which were two tasks I'd mastered very early on in my recovery. However, as time had passed, I'd also managed to put the hairdryer and straighteners plugs in and out of the socket too, as my fine motor control and strength had improved also.

Managing to shower independently was a massive accomplishment for me, restoring some of my dignity. Yes, I still needed help to get my clothes on in the morning and get my prosthetic legs on, but being able to not feel exposed and have my underwear on, when my carer arrived

felt so good. Kim was concerned that what I was doing was too dangerous, and I was putting myself at risk of falling. But transferring from
my wheelchair to the toilet seat without my legs, was even more risky
and I did that every day. However, I knew I had to keep myself safe, so I
took my mobile phone into the wet room with me and made sure that I
wasn't in the house on my own when I had a shower.

Another achievement during October was to use my sewing machine
yet again. This time, I put the hems up on two pairs of trousers which
I had purchased, but were too long for me. It was good to be able to
do this on my own, just as I'd done in the past, when using my sewing
machine was an everyday occurrence. I knew I had a long way to go
before I could achieve being able to trim material and being realistic, I
knew that I might never achieve that.

I received my appointment at WestMARC regarding my bionic arm
and my big brother accompanied me through to Glasgow. It was fasci-
nating how I was able to open and shut a bionic hand to allocate the
nerves in my left stump by pressing the transmitter plates against my
inner and outer arm. My arm was cast, then marked at the best positions
for the plates to pick up my nerve signals. There will be one or two more
appointments to try on the arm and make sure it is working effectively.
To begin with it will be made of see-through plastic. Once the arm is
deemed ready to be made into a prosthetic material, it will be a matter
of weeks before I receive the finished product. So for now, I must wait
patiently. But knowing that I am going to receive my bionic arm soon,
is good enough for now.

I reached my full potential at physio and the work I was doing with
Kerry, such as using the exercise bike, could be done out with the physiotherapy department. I'd recognised it was now time for me to move on,
but I also was aware that I had to have something else in place to enable
me to continue exercising and to maintain my strength and fitness levels.
But I also needed to continue in order to have some sense of routine in
my life, able to get out of the house and interact with others, instead of
becoming socially isolated.

But in order to do that, I needed to be able to access facilities I could
manage with my distinctive disability needs - something that I felt

comfortable and confident in doing and hopefully as independently as was realistically possible. To this end, Kerry contacted Active Options, and she accompanied me to a meeting with their representative at my local Leisure Centre, where my capabilities in the multi-gym were assessed. I managed to use six pieces of equipment, including the exercise bike and the treadmill. With my bionic arm, I will be able to use more of the equipment on offer. It meant that I would be able to use the gym independently and my friend, who had accompanied me to the meeting, agreed to come along too.

Accessing the gym, meant my journey with Kerry was coming to an end. Thinking of my life without her support was unimaginable and scary. I felt I was losing another limb and I didn't know how I was going to cope without her. She had been my consistent support throughout my journey. Her ability to help me remain strong and push myself physically and mentally and never give in, making me rise to challenge after challenge and succeed, I knew could never be replicated by anyone else. She had never once let me down and would go the extra mile to help me, even beyond her role of being my physio. I know that even though she will no longer be my physio, she will forever be my friend and we will remain in contact.

Even although I achieved massive goals during October and learned that I was ready for a bionic arm, I was still struggling emotionally. I couldn't understand why I felt worse now than I had ever been throughout my journey. In discussing this with Lynne, crying throughout most of my appointment, she helped me to understand that it was because I now realised the reality of it all and I wasn't coping with facing up to what that meant and how that was never going to change. Although I had lost my limbs twenty months ago, I was still grieving for the person I once was and recognised that I possibly always would do.

I often felt a fraud, as I knew I portrayed to the outside world, someone who was coping well, when in fact I was often struggling to remain positive. My personality meant that I'd protect others from feeling uncomfortable around me, but in doing this, I wasn't being honest in how I was really feeling. I was a dab hand at telling people when they asked me how I was, that I was fine. But I really wasn't. It also meant I was keeping all my frustrations, emotions and feelings to myself, heightening my anxiety and stress levels. Some of the strategies used to relieve stress were to do things like squeezing a stress ball, punching a pillow, going for a walk or a run, or even putting the music up high and dancing around the room. How could I do any of these things without my arms and legs?

Speaking openly and honestly to Lynne, I was able to tell her how I so wished that I could run away at times and be somewhere on my own, away from the reality of living without limbs. But running away would not help me. I would have to take my reality with me. Nor could I go on my own, as I need support on a daily basis. The relentless impact of my disabilities on my day-to-day activities was constantly in my face. I could no longer live my life like everybody else. I couldn't be impulsive and go on a last-minute bargain holiday, just because I wanted to. I couldn't jump in the car myself and drive anywhere I fancied. I could go on and on naming impulsive things I couldn't do, but what was the point, as it was too upsetting to think about and for that to change, I would have to grow my legs and arms back.

I think that the thought of the on-coming winter and what that meant for me, was another reason for my low mood. Rain, frost and snow would curtail my ability to get outdoors, and the dark nights would make the days seem even longer.

At the end of October, it had been twenty months since I had contracted sepsis. Although I was struggling, I knew I had come so far on my journey of recovery, having achieved more than I or anyone else could ever have imagined. I was now living in my new home, which has given me the ability to build on being as independent as I can be. It's not quite finished yet, but it soon will be, and next summer, I am looking forward to the luxury of sitting outside in my back garden.

I know I will continue to try and achieve more, but I recognise that there are some things I'll never achieve, like putting my legs on or my earrings and jewellery. I also know that no matter what I achieve in the future, if I'm unable to wear my prosthetic legs, whether due to my stumps being sore, issues with the legs themselves, or in the event of me being unwell, then I'm back to being unable to do very little for myself.

and that will happen at times.

I know I need to try and accept the reality of it all and I know that isn't going to be right now, as I'm not ready to accept it yet. Maybe I never will. What happened to me is too big for me to understand, never mind accept. I still find myself remembering events of the early days of my illness when I was so very ill and I find it all very confusing. I often wonder why I continue to look back, but it's probably because, what happened to me was too horrific and so unimaginable for me to accept and as a result of this, I might never stop thinking about the events that took place during that time.

But, for now, I'm taking each day as it comes, facing the challenges that I have to face. I hope that one day, I'll get used to living as a quadruple amputee. Maybe then, I'll be able to stop grieving for the life I had and concentrate on making the most of the life I have now.

An ambulance driver taking me to physio one day asked me how my book could have an ending, as my story is never ending. He was so right. My life is never going to be easy and there will be lots of barriers along the way, ones that I will have to tackle. I will always continue to strive to set myself goals and work towards achieving them in order that my life has a purpose and is fulfilling and worthwhile. I will have

days when I'll think, 'What's the point?' and days when I will feel good. I'm well aware of that.

There will always be the question 'What happens next?' and the answer is, 'I'll just have to wait and see.'

THE END

Since the completion of this book, things have continued to move on for me. I have received my bionic arm. I know it will take lots of practice before I'm skilful at using it, but I already recognise the positive impact it will have on my ability to do tasks, particularly in the kitchen environment. I have also received the legs that I can wear whilst in the shower and was able to stand in my shower for the first time since February 2018. A massive event for me. You have no idea how that felt, standing under the water, as I used to do when I had my limbs and how emotional it made me feel. It's scary standing in water, with me frightened that I'll slip, but I'm hoping that I'll become more confidant in them. Having them will also allow me to access a normal shower cubicle, when I'm staying away from home. Mind you packing a pair of legs to take with me, along with my toilet bag is hard to comprehend, emphasising that my new normal is anything but normal and something I never thought in my wildest dreams I'd ever be doing.

My new legs with flexible ankles are also in the process of being made and I hope to get them in the near future. I am sure these new limbs will make a tremendous difference in my ability to walk more confidently, particularly when outside on uneven surfaces. My goal then is to walk more, going to Emma's, my brothers' and friends' houses nearby, without being in my wheelchair.

My road to achieving a happy, independent, purposeful and fulfilling life continues.

EPILOGUE

I have worried at times that the book's content comes across as too upsetting and negative, but to change it would have meant that I wouldn't have been honest about how it really is for me. I wanted to tell my story truthfully, hence the title, 'RAW & REAL.'

Writing my book has been a journey of its own, stirring many emotions, on a regular basis, that sometimes were very hard to cope with and at times made me feel like giving up. Writing about what happened highlighted how shocking the experience really was and I couldn't help but ask myself how I'd managed to cope with it all. I also recognised how hard the experience has been for my family, and friends, and I can't help feeling guilty for that, even though I had no control over what happened.

My journey from the beginning has had many ups and downs and I coped better than I could ever have imagined. Even so, it would often have been so easy for me to stay in bed on many mornings, as living without my limbs is so hard. Every day is challenging, with every task requiring so much energy and strength. But I make myself get up, and I keep rising to the challenges of each day. I know that giving in is not an option.

I am challenged every time I go out in public, as people stare, but I'm getting better at ignoring it. When I am in my wheelchair, I hate when people talk to the person who is with me, rather than talk to me. Sometimes they talk to me as though they are talking to a child. I've lost my limbs, not my brain. I've noticed that often when I bump into people I know, and they are seeing me for the first time since my amputations, they tell me I'm looking well, then add, "Your hair's nice!" Is this because they don't want to focus on the rest of my body, with its missing limbs and don't know what else to say?

All I know, is that I have to rise above other people's reactions to me, as if I don't, I'd never go out in public and I can't afford to do that.

Losing my identity and everything that represented me as a person, has been so hard for me to deal with. I am still trying hard to find the new me, but I won't give up on that one.

I've also struggled with losing my ability to do the job I loved and I still find it hard to think about how upsetting it was for me to cope with the circumstances in which my working life ended.

My fight-back could only be achieved by putting myself first and that was so out of character for me. I needed people to listen to my needs and understand that my decisions were the right ones for me. How else could I cope and try to make a new future for myself? Unfortunately, this approach led to me losing one of my close family members, who instead of listening and giving me the support, I needed, caused me anxiety and stress. It led to the breakdown of our relationship, which can never be repaired. It was another loss to add to all the other losses I'd endured, but one that could have been avoided and that is so sad.

However, on a positive note, I am so lucky to have two amazing daughters and a son-in-law, who have made it their goal to make my life as good as it can be. Having my two granddaughters in my life reminds me every day of how lucky I am, to have survived sepsis and be able to see them grow up.

I have an amazing family who are there for me whenever I need them. My friends have been by my side over the last twenty months and I so appreciate their commitment to me. Even friends I had lost touch with are now back in my life and that is something to be grateful for.

Another positive outcome is that I have come to appreciate what a wonderful and caring community I live in. Over the years, I have attended many of the wide-ranging activities which our very active community groups have organised, but I found their support and generosity phenomenal and so appreciated.

I also want to thank the amazing staff of Ward 33 at Kirkcaldy Victoria

Hospital. They were there for me every step of the way, and without their dedication and support, I know I wouldn't have coped as I did. They helped me find my sense of humour again. I needed humour to keep me strong and realistic.

*

The amazing and dedicated support I've received from so many individuals at the hospital has been so appreciated, with there being too many to name. I'd like to thank each and every one of them, for helping me get to where I am today. They know who they are! There are two people in particular, who have continued to support me throughout my journey - Lynne, thank you for getting to know me and being with me through each stage of my emotional roller coaster, helping me remain positive and continue to never give up. Kerry - my rock, the person who never gave up on me and helped me learn to walk again. No words can explain how much I appreciate all you've done for me. Saying thank you, doesn't come close.

In writing this book, I hope I have highlighted the effects contracting sepsis can cause and how serious this condition is. Around fifty-two thousand people in the UK die every year from this illness, more than the total amount of deaths from breast cancer, prostate cancer and bowel cancer. Throughout the world, someone dies from sepsis every three point five seconds, claiming six million lives a year, and we need to be aware of this. These figures don't include those who survive, like myself. If telling my story can raise awareness of the need for early identification of the symptoms of sepsis and of the consequent need for urgent action, and even save just one person's life, then writing this book will have been worthwhile.

I survived and I'm a survivor. Contracting sepsis and my journey thereafter has changed me forever, and not just physically. My priorities and values have changed. I don't dwell on silly issues that are not important. I focus on what really matters - being happy, healthy, having a purpose in life and most importantly, spending time with the people I love. Money and possessions are now way down my list of priorities.

I don't like being half the person that I was physically, but I do like ME and the person I've become. I have been through the most horrific and life changing experience imaginable and I believe I have shown strength beyond my comprehension. No matter what I've had thrown at me during this journey, I have kept fighting and never given up. I know I never will, as that's not an option.

My life was saved by the swift actions of my son-in-law, taking me to hospital when he did, and the dedicated staff in A&E and ICU at Kirkcaldy Victoria Hospital, who, although recognising, I was more than likely going to die, continued in their efforts to try and save my life. I owe it to them to embrace the fact that I'm alive and kicking, and although my life is so much different to the life I had before, it's a precious gift that I won't take for granted.

Dear Reader

Thank you for reading my story. Never in my wildest dreams, did I ever think I'd write a book, but it seemed the natural thing to do, after the unimaginable experience I've been through.

My hope, is that by you reading my story, it will highlight the need for you to seek medical help as soon as possible if you ever think you may have Sepsis, as early intervention could save your life, or prevent lifelong medical conditions, like my own. I also encourage you to let everyone you care about know how serious and life-threatening Sepsis is. If it happened to me through sustaining a small paper cut, it can happen to anybody.

I also hope that my story highlights the need to challenge diversity and never give in, as what is the alternative? Yes, this can be hard to achieve at times, but I did it, so you can too if the need should ever arise.

Below are the contact details for the Sepsis Trust and the Signs and Symptoms of Sepsis.

Sepsis Trust; https://sepsistrust.org

Signs and Symptoms

    S – Shivery, fever or very cold

    E – Extreme pain or general discomfort

    P – Pale or discoloured skin

    S – Sleepy, difficult to rouse, confused

    I – "I feel I might die"

    S – Short of breath

Lastly, please can you help me promote my book by leaving a review in Amazon or Good Reads.

Kind Regards

Marguerite

Email Address: margueriteauthor@gmail.com